KU-733-006

A Table for One

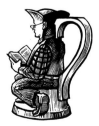

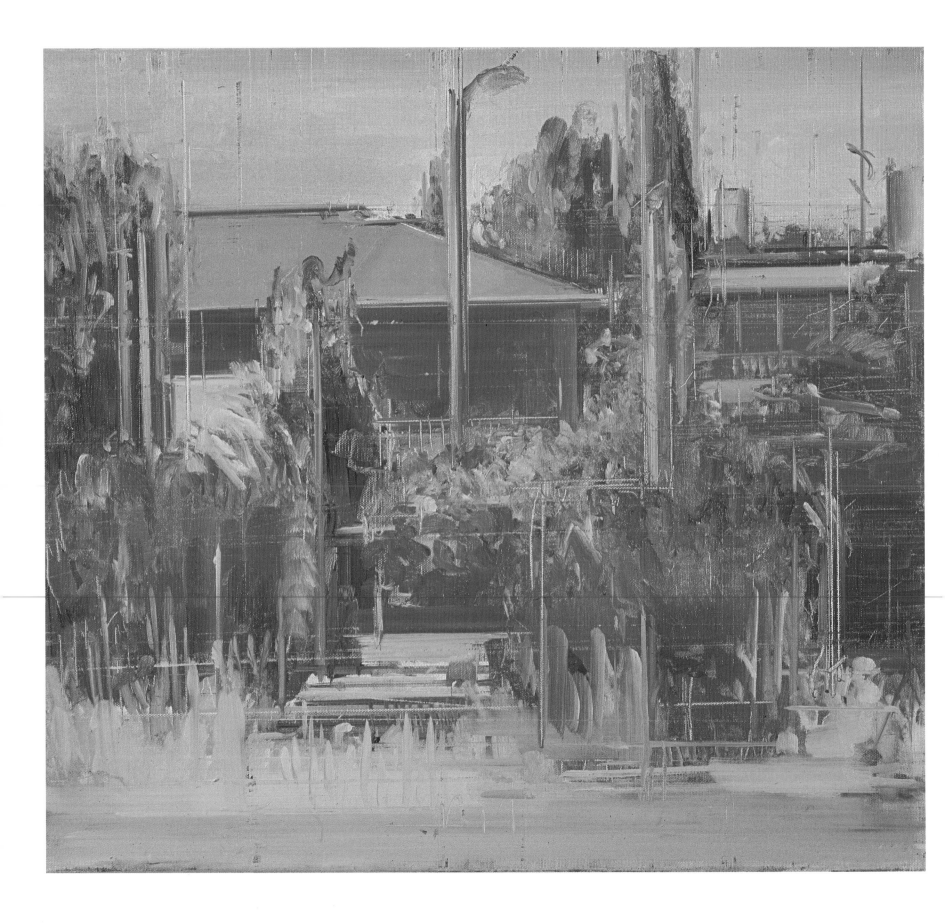

Aharon Appelfeld
Meir Appelfeld

A TABLE FOR ONE
Under the Light of Jerusalem

TRANSLATED FROM THE HEBREW BY
Aloma Halter

The Toby Press

CUMBRIA COUNTY LIBRARY	
H J	14/11/2005
956.944	£19.99

A Table for One
First English Language Edition 2005

The Toby Press LLC, 2005
POB 8531, New Milford, CT. 06676-8531, USA
& POB 2455, London W1A 5WY, England
www.tobypress.com

First published as *Od Hayom Gadol*
Copyright © 2001 Aharon Appelfeld
Paintings and Drawings © 2005 Meir Appelfeld
All rights reserved

Translation by Aloma Halter © *The* Toby Press LLC, 2004

The right of Aharon Appelfeld to be identified as the
author of this work has been asserted by him in accordance
with the Copyright, Designs & Patents Act, 1988.

All rights reserved. No part of this publication may be
reproduced, stored in a retrieval system, or transmitted
in any form or by any means, electronic, mechanical,
photocopying or otherwise, without the prior
permission of the publisher, except in the case of brief
quotations embodied in critical articles or reviews.

ISBN 1 59264 110 5, *hardcover*

A CIP catalogue record for this title is
available from the British Library

Book designed by Tani Bayer © *The* Toby Press LLC, 2005
Photographs of paintings and drawings by Yoram Lehmann

Typeset in Brioso Pro by Jerusalem Typesetting

Printed in Israel

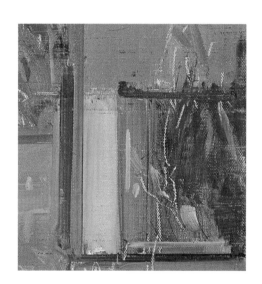

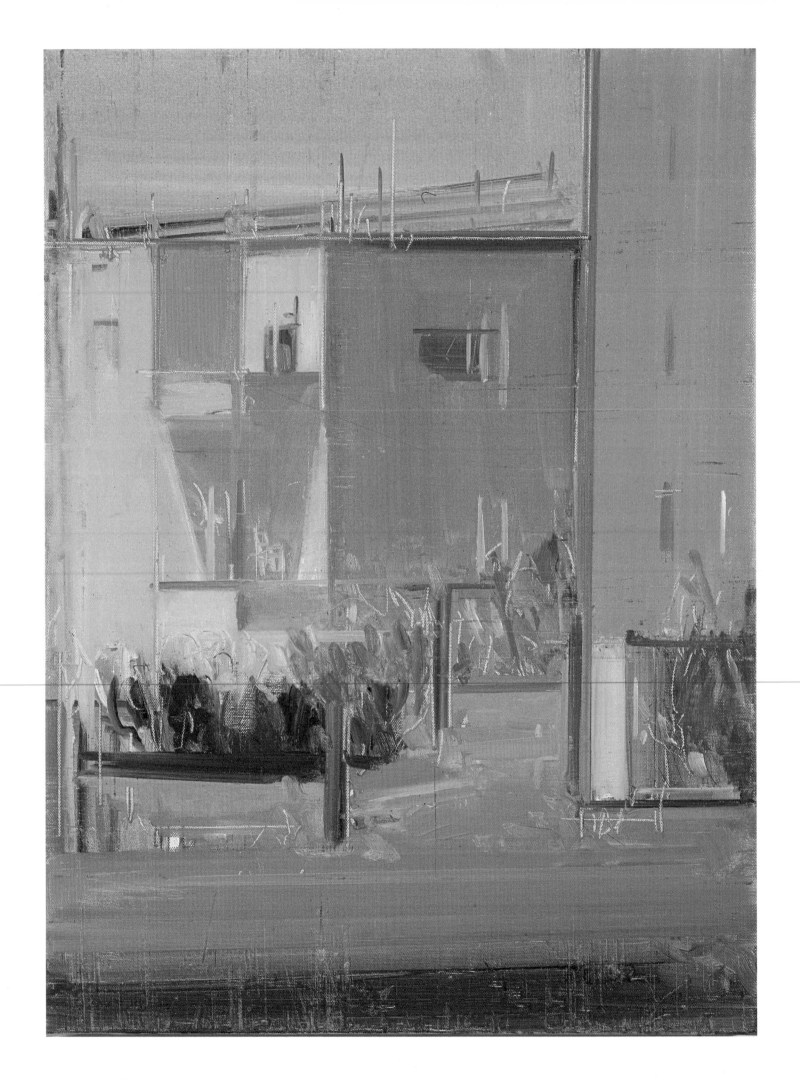

CHAPTER ONE

I have lived in Jerusalem since the age of fourteen, for almost sixty years. When I ask myself where I've spent the most time and the happiest hours throughout these years, I have to admit that it's in cafés. A café is my lookout, my place of observation; on certain days my refuge. In periods when I'm inspired, it's the place where I'm best able to concentrate. My room at home is quiet and secluded, but sometimes it's hard to concentrate there, or I get lazy, distracted, my mind wanders and I end up sitting on the sofa and leafing through a book.

My attraction to cafés probably goes back to the beautiful cafés of Czernowitz, in Bukovina, where I was born. The cafés there were full but not crowded. Those who frequented the Czernowitz cafés had their regular places, zealously kept for them by the waiters. Naturally, the tables by the windows were the most sought after. Every regular had his own spot. In contrast to the pubs, the cafés were quiet, circumspect, more like public libraries—everyone immersed in his own newspaper or book. The conversations, even the arguments, were not loud. These cafés of my childhood were distinguished by their secluded niches for chess. People sat for hours poring over the chessboards, as if the entire world hung in the balance. My father was an excellent chess player. When he would play, people would gather around our table, intently following the moves.

When I grew up and needed time to myself, I went to cafés. During the 1950s and 1960s, Jerusalem cafés were still quiet, there was no music, and they retained something of the aromas and manners of European cafés. They were all like this: Café Rehavia in Jerusalem's garden suburb in the center of the city, Café Atara on Ben-Yehuda Street, Café Vienna on Jaffa Street, or Café Hermon on Keren Kayemet. Not one of them is there any more.

What is it about a café that makes it such a wonderful place to concentrate? Perhaps here it should be said—most cafés nowadays are not so much cafés but more like large, crowded spaces invaded with violent music. Don't try to find any quiet there, or something mysterious, or that furtive connection with those surrounding you. It's only a nexus, a point of transition, a place where you wait impatiently. Cafés of this sort are not inviting, nor are they intended for sitting or lingering. You'd like to get out of them as quickly as possible. Real cafés are inviting, they tempt you with fresh coffee and a cake straight out of the oven, and offer the chance to spend a precious hour or two alone with yourself.

A café is not a sentimental place. Those who sit in cafés are generally people who find their own homes cramped, or for whom loneliness is a frequent companion, people from foreign parts who have gathered so they can speak their native tongue and share memories. In cafés you can sometimes hear words cold as ice, or words full of longing and a fierce loyalty. Usually there's silence in a café, but sometimes a wave of speech will surge up, flooding the listener with painful things that have been mostly kept down, things buried deep in the soul for many years that have at last found an opening and emerged in words.

There are times I feel that a café is a port to which all gates of the imagination are open. You sail toward distant lands, you are again

CHAPTER TWO

Café Peter in the German Colony was my first regular café. I used to go there for more than ten years, from 1953 till the mid-1960s. It was in its garden that I began my university studies and there that I completed them. The dark, narrow little room that I rented in Rehavia was just a place to sleep; I ate my meals at Café Peter, read, prepared for the examinations—but mostly I wrote there. To be more accurate, it was where I struggled to find my voice.

with people you loved. Toward evening, a café can resemble a secular prayer house in which people are immersed in observation.

I like being in a café in the winter. Winter imparts a lot of flavor to a cup of hot coffee. In winter, the people whom I wait for emerge from their hiding places. Sometimes it might be a man who resembles my uncle, and sometimes it's the splitting image of a beloved woman who has passed away. Once a woman who looked like my mother came into the café. In winter, the imagination has more strength: the heart is open and receptive, the words you need are ready and you can recall things that had been hidden from you as well. It's assumed that cafés are better for writing poetry than writing prose. I find that the groundswell of noise in a café stimulates me to grasp what is most important. Often the quiet at home can lead me astray and into inessential details. Because of their rhythm, cafés push me to choose the essential.

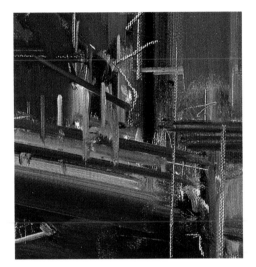

The dream of becoming a writer had stayed with me since my discharge from the army. I said "dream," but it would be better to say "delusion" and even self-deception. In my parents' home in Czernowitz, I had finished first grade, but the war broke out at the end of that school year. In Israel, I studied for about two and a half years in the Youth Aliyah, and after that I did my army service. I completed my matriculation exams without any assistance: I bought used and stained textbooks for next to nothing, and got hold of a few notes from high school students. Algebra and trigonometry presented the biggest obstacles: I took the exam three times, and only passed on the third try.

I have written all my novels in Jerusalem cafés. When I'm abroad, I may jot things down, edit a page or even a chapter, but I've never completed a short story or a novel abroad. Only in a Jerusalem café do I feel the freedom of imagination. That's my starting point. That's where I depart from and it is to there that I return. There were many houses and fields and streams in the region of my childhood, but to reach them I need a home port.

That was my education—or rather my lack of education. It was with this meager equipment that I sought to become a writer. Though six years of war taught me many important life-lessons, you can't get far without any linguistic or cultural tools. My mother tongue was German. My grandparents spoke Yiddish. We lived among Ruthenian peasants and so we spoke Ruthenian.

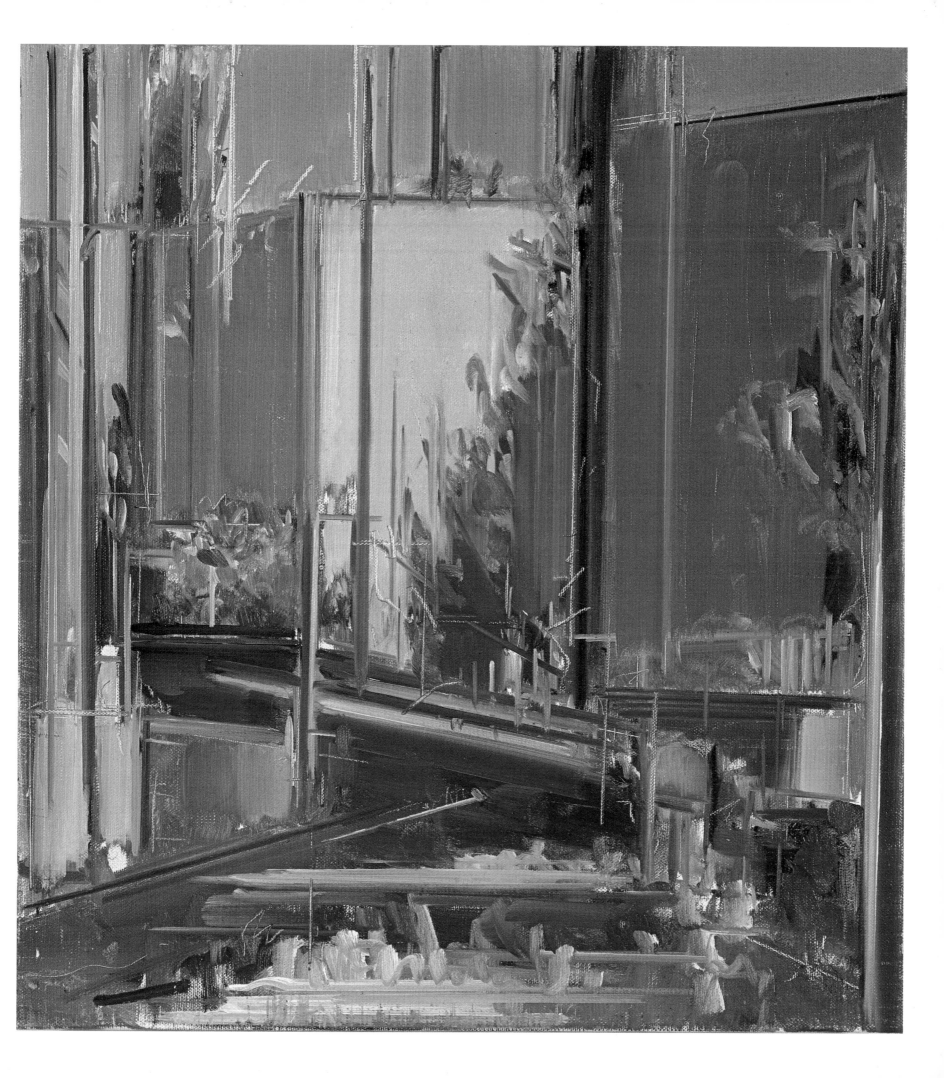

The government was Romanian, so we spoke Romanian. The intelligentsia often spoke French, so we spoke French. After the war I was with the Russians and I learned to speak Russian. Those languages that were not too deeply rooted in me rapidly faded in Israel; however, Hebrew had not yet taken root in my soul. To try to link my experience to the few Hebrew words at my disposal was too much of a stretch. But I'm rushing ahead.

Before I dreamed of being a writer, I had a different vision: being an Israeli, looking like an Israeli and behaving like one. All through the years in the Youth Aliyah and in the army I nurtured this illusion. It found expression, among other things, in jogging at night, working out, lifting weights, and various kinds of unpleasant physical exertions. But all this seemed to have no effect on my height, the way I walked, or the way I spoke. My shyness never disappeared, and I still spoke haltingly. Several of my friends in the Youth Aliyah did change—they did assimilate and when they were called up to the army, they were accepted into elite units. But it was as if my body refused to change, and even my interior, apparently, insisted on remaining what it had been. Our desires, even the strongest ones, seldom dictate what we actually do.

What I couldn't bring about in life, I tried to do in writing. After failed attempts at poetry, I tried to write about my life in Israel. It was no less awful than the sentimental poems that I had been writing. Strange how what we want befuddles us; to what extent we are in fact hostage to our desires. It is only the fortunate few who, from the outset, recognize the path that fate has marked out for them.

As I said, Café Peter was a home to me; if truth be told, it was more than a home. All that I hazily remembered was revealed to me in the shape of living people, who spoke in tones that reminded me of home and who, between one conversation and another, might let drop a word about the ghetto or the camp.

The people who frequented Café Peter in those years had come

from Transylvania, Hungary, Bukovina, and Bulgaria; they spoke the languages of the Austro-Hungarian Empire, particularly German. Everything there—the taste of food, the manners, the tone of speech, the silence between the sentences—was just as it had been at home. The garden too—the huge atrium, the sideboards, and the chairs—all these were as if they had been reincarnated from "there" and had come here.

I don't remember who first brought me to Café Peter, but I do recall that no sooner was I through the doorway, then I knew that these people were my lost uncles and cousins, they had brought their language here with them—their attire, their little shops in the pastoral villages, and their splendid department stores from the towns from which they had been uprooted.

I had already been in Israel for some seven years, yet only now had I returned home. I was so enchanted by the place that whenever I had a spare hour I would rush over, and sit there spellbound. I understood everything that was said around the little tables, not only the words, but also what was implied, the hints and the silences. I immediately felt that these people, whose names I didn't know, were my real relatives. It was as if everything that had surrounded me up to now didn't touch my real essence. That essence was embodied by these émigrés, who spoke Hapsburg German, who had been uprooted from the land of their birth and now found themselves lost in their homeland. To assuage that loss, they would gather together, evoking and reminiscing about their homes and their fields.

One autumn night, I heard one of them confess that the years in the labor camp were a time when all reserves, body and soul, had been drawn upon, yet they were years of hope and immense belief. Since the Liberation, it was as if everything had been overturned: now it was hard to sleep at night, and torturous thoughts returned with piercing intensity—the body's betrayal. The restraint in his voice shocked me. Yet strange as it was, no one contradicted him.

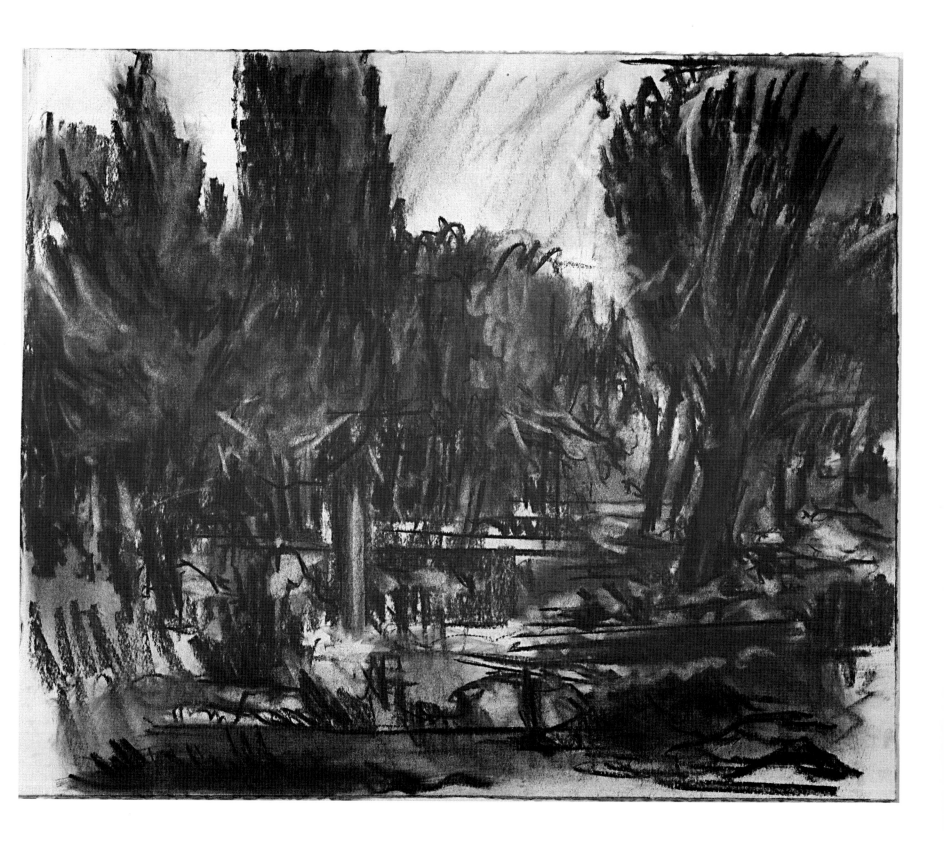

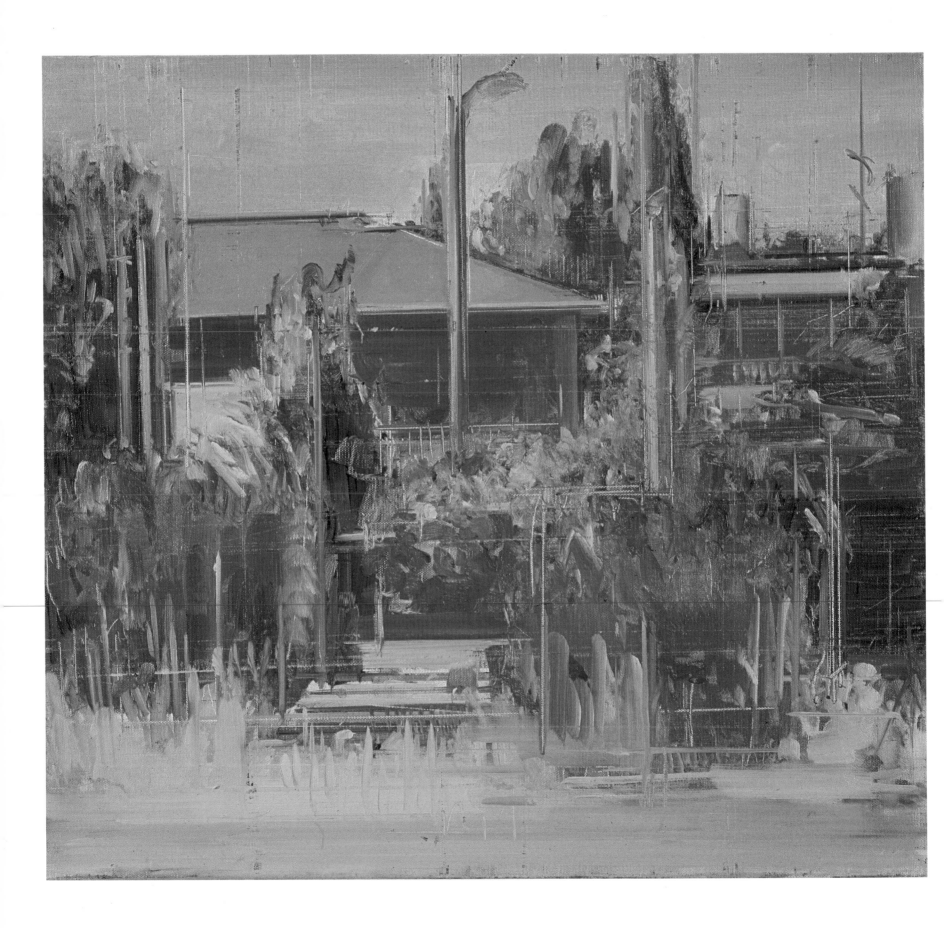

CHAPTER THREE

Café Peter was my great discovery. It was at Café Peter that, once and for all, I gave up on the dream of becoming what I could never become; it was there that I stopped trying to belong to something I simply didn't belong to. After all, my homeland was not the land of the Hebrew revolution, but the land of émigrés. This discovery did not come to me overnight—time, humility, and the renunciation of great ambitions, were all required.

The émigré is not a loveable personality. Usually, he's a man who has left half of his life behind him, everything that was built up so carefully is gone, and his loved ones have been brutally murdered. You look at him and you can read his entire life in his body. At Café Peter, I learned to look carefully at the human body, its positions, its movements; a body tells you far more than words like "loneliness" and "sorrow."

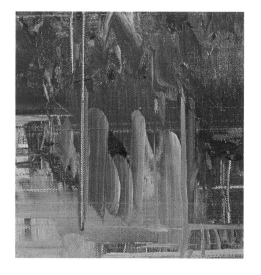

I have to confess today: there were years in Israel that I distanced myself from survivors, I avoided them, I did everything in order not to be near them. They were called "the Desert Generation," or "the dregs of humanity." Survivors embodied the nakedness of exile, the wanderings, the Holocaust. Like many others, I also did not wish to belong to them, to speak their language, or to be linked to their memories. Yet suddenly I discovered them in the garden of Café Peter, no different from anyone else. They talked about a certain apartment that was cold in winter, they talked about bookshelves that they had left in some far-off place—they spoke about things that *could* be spoken of. When it came to pain that was really deep—they were silent.

The 1940s and 1950s were years when lofty words abounded in Israel. Yet in this café, people spoke in the way we used to speak to one another, directly and without pathos. It was at Café Peter that I wrote the short story "Berta" in 1958. It portrays the change and the turning point that took place in me; not to write about the "new Jew" and not about the idyll of working the land in Israel, but about people who had been in places that I was in and ended up here. At Café Peter I learned how to listen to speech, to distinguish between what was spoken and what was unspoken; about what it was possible to speak of and about what was forbidden. At Café Peter, I became aware of myself and the people around me. There I learned what an effect suffering can have: it does not only bring ugliness and shallowness.

Almost every morning at half past then, Tina's friends would bring her to Café Peter. She sat in a wheelchair, very erect, her face radiant. From the very first time I saw her, I never once heard her utter a complaint. She was interested, asked questions, but about herself—not one word.

A pharmacist by profession, she also knew a lot about medicine, psychology, and literature. An avid reader, she would draw her friends into everything she read. Over the years, I pieced together the details of her life: After she had completed her pharmaceutical studies, she had worked for two years in a little town next to Kosice, in Transylvania. Seven months before the end of the war she was caught and sent to Auschwitz. A few days before the Liberation, she tripped, falling from the train carriage on which she was loading crates of canned goods. Had it not been for her friends who

CHAPTER FOUR

took care of her, she wouldn't have made it. Since then, her friends have been with her, and she with them.

When you ask Tina something, she raises her head to listen. Before she answers, she'll ask for more details. She usually responds in just a sentence or two. When one of her friends tells something of her life, she bends her head. Everyone here is injured to some extent, and people chose their words with great caution. Sometimes a word escapes and suddenly everyone becomes quiet.

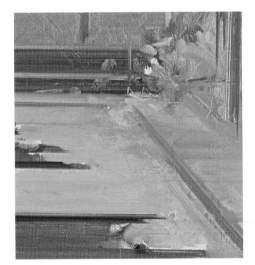

I notice that Tina is always in good spirits. On more than one occasion, I've seen her biting her lips, probably from the pain, but to someone looking at her from close up, it looks like an intellectual effort. Her friends who've brought her to Israel love her, but other people, even complete strangers, also love her. Whenever she comes, they're happy to see her. Once I heard her say: "I can drink without sugar, too." In her voice I heard not only renunciation and acceptance, but also a readiness to live her injured life.

"The émigré is without dignity—he's evasive: when he's called up for military service, he shirks responsibility. Émigrés do their army service in the canteen." I heard things like this occasionally. I even internalized them. With what ease we take in words of criticism; sometimes we even believe it ourselves. I got to know Tina and people like her and I knew that suffering not only turns people into ugly and selfish creatures, but it can purify and refine the soul. An injured person can also be a noble person.

Café Peter was my first school for writing. There I learned that simple words are the precise ones, and that daily life is our most true expression. During the 1950s, young authors wrote in very high-flown language, either imitating the ancient texts or inventing a convoluted style. I was also drawn to these lofty expressions. But whenever I sat next to my brothers, refugees like myself, I saw that life's mysteries should be clothed in facts. The simple and the factual lead to truth. An excess of words can be a serious obstacle. Another important lesson from my brother refugees is to see the essence and be sparing. What you don't have to say, shouldn't be said.

Everyone at Café Peter carried a cruel country in his soul, a home that had been broken into, and people from whom they would never part. How does one go on living with this in dignity? They actually didn't discuss those "big" issues, but talked about practical matters. One of the useful unwritten rules was: A man should not talk about himself unless it carries some meaning for others. To speak about yourself just because something has happened to you is foolishness, or worse still, pure selfishness. For years I sat near them, and every day absorbed a tiny fragment of their soul. Maybe it would be more accurate to say that they were in me.

"How do you feel, Tina?" someone asked the woman in the wheelchair. Tina opened wide her large eyes and she said, "I feel good."

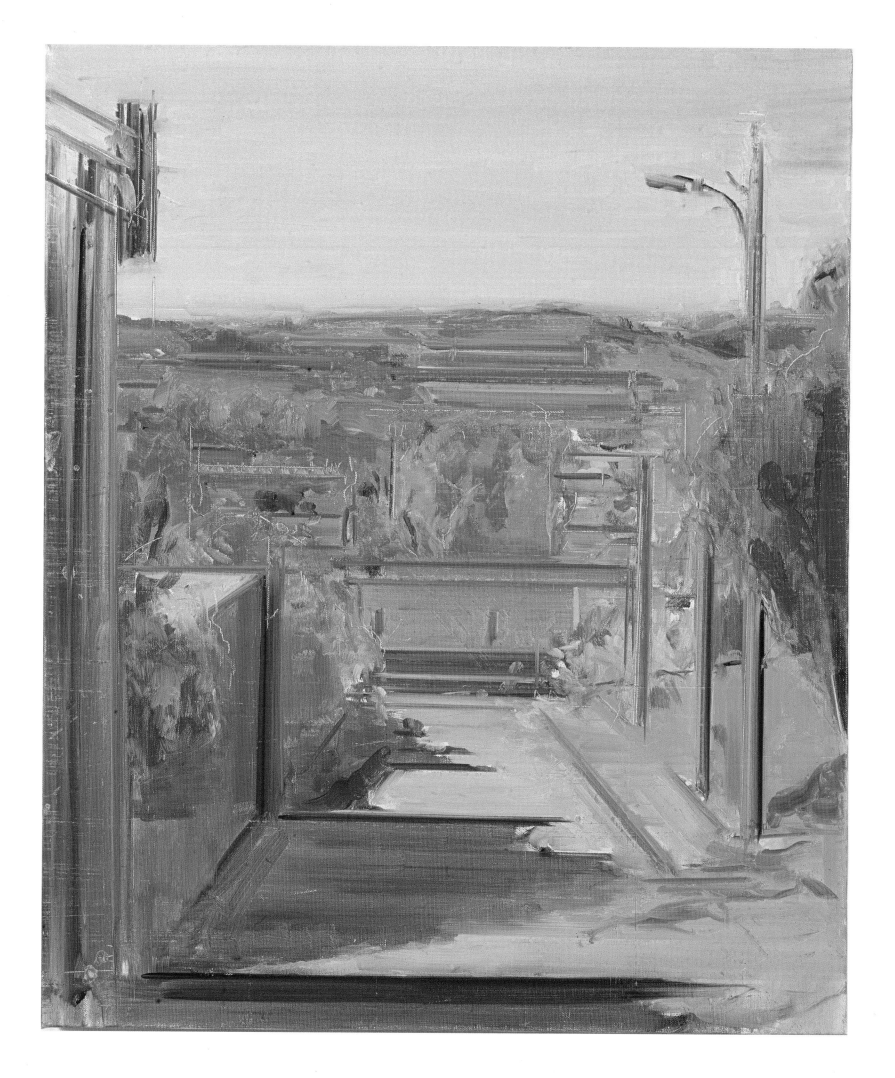

It was at Café Peter that I learned the principles of my art. Later, at other cafés, I added knowledge and experience, but it was at Café Peter that my writing took shape, and it was there that I wrote my first books. On several occasions I asked myself what place there could be for low-key literature like mine in a country that was entirely ideological, full of words and arguments and counter arguments; a country that spewed out words like a machine. A country where any nuance would be trodden underfoot, and where people were continually asking: "Are you with us or against us?" In such a country, is there a place for writing like mine?

It turns out that my fears were exaggerated. When my first book, *Smoke*, appeared in 1962, it was well received. Most praised it, and there were also those who criticized it. I was happy for the good words, but in my heart I knew that there was still a long road ahead of me.

A question on one's appearance immediately draws close attention. People, even those who aren't particularly careful about how they look, are still sensitive about their appearance. They don't like to appear weak or sick. They have brought this fear with them from *there*, and it is betrayed in the hesitancy of the answer. I paid attention: a question about how one's night had been was usually met with positive descriptions: "good", "not bad". It wasn't that complaints were out of the question, but rather that they were few and usually well camouflaged. Pain is not something easily shared with other people.

Not everyone is as well educated as Tina. Arthur had a large general store in a village in the middle of the Transylvanian countryside, a kind of supermarket, long before "supermarkets" came into fashion. He was a tall man and broad—from his appearance, one could guess the dimensions of the store. Alongside this giant, everyone looked skinny, short, and puny. His appearance was in sharp contrast to his character—reticent and shy, he would barely utter a word. But he was a master listener, and when he listened, his whole giant body listened. Such close attentiveness was not at all arrogant or mocking, as one might have expected. There was a kind of wonder in his attentiveness, as if everyone were his children or younger brothers to be encouraged.

Despite Arthur's height and his solidity, and despite what he had been through in life, he was full of naiveté. Served a sandwich decorated by vegetables, he could be delighted. He was very fond of children, though he wouldn't pick up a baby so as not to scare it. He would bend down to the stroller and make funny noises.

During the war he had escaped from a labor camp disguised as a chimney sweep, and that's how he managed to survive. Not a single member of his large family had survived. He was completely alone in Israel; his "family" were those people who surrounded him at Café Peter. He helped everyone, even the woman who owned the place. When they needed to move a table or an oven, he would do it with the alacrity of a young man.

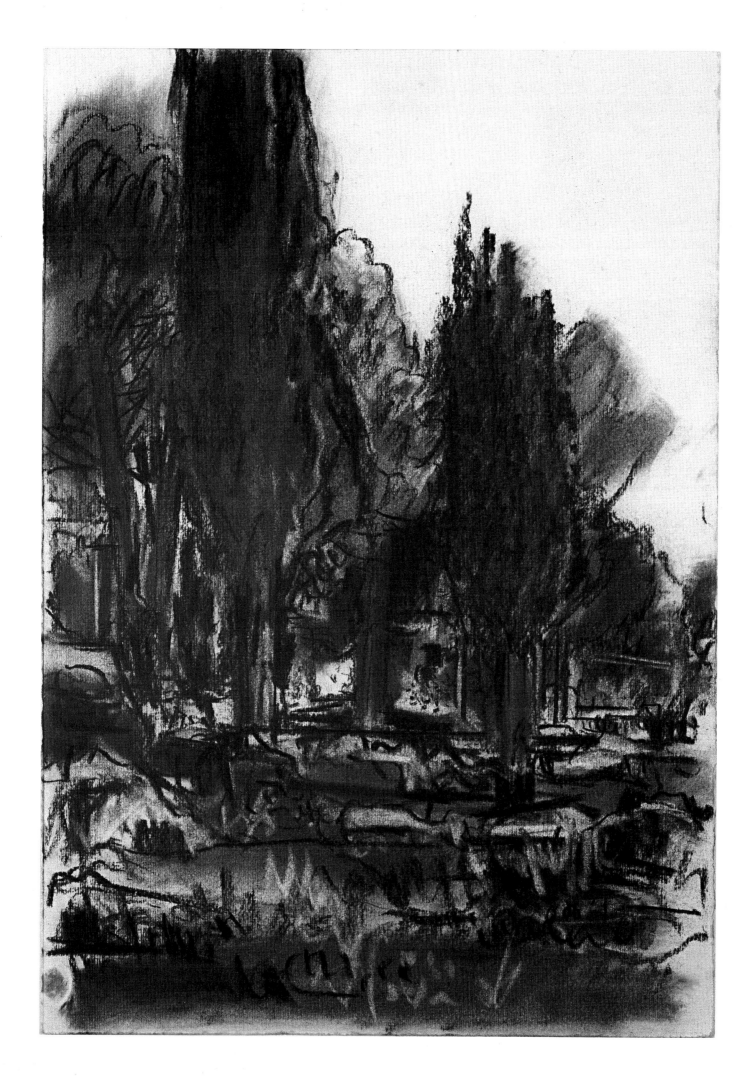

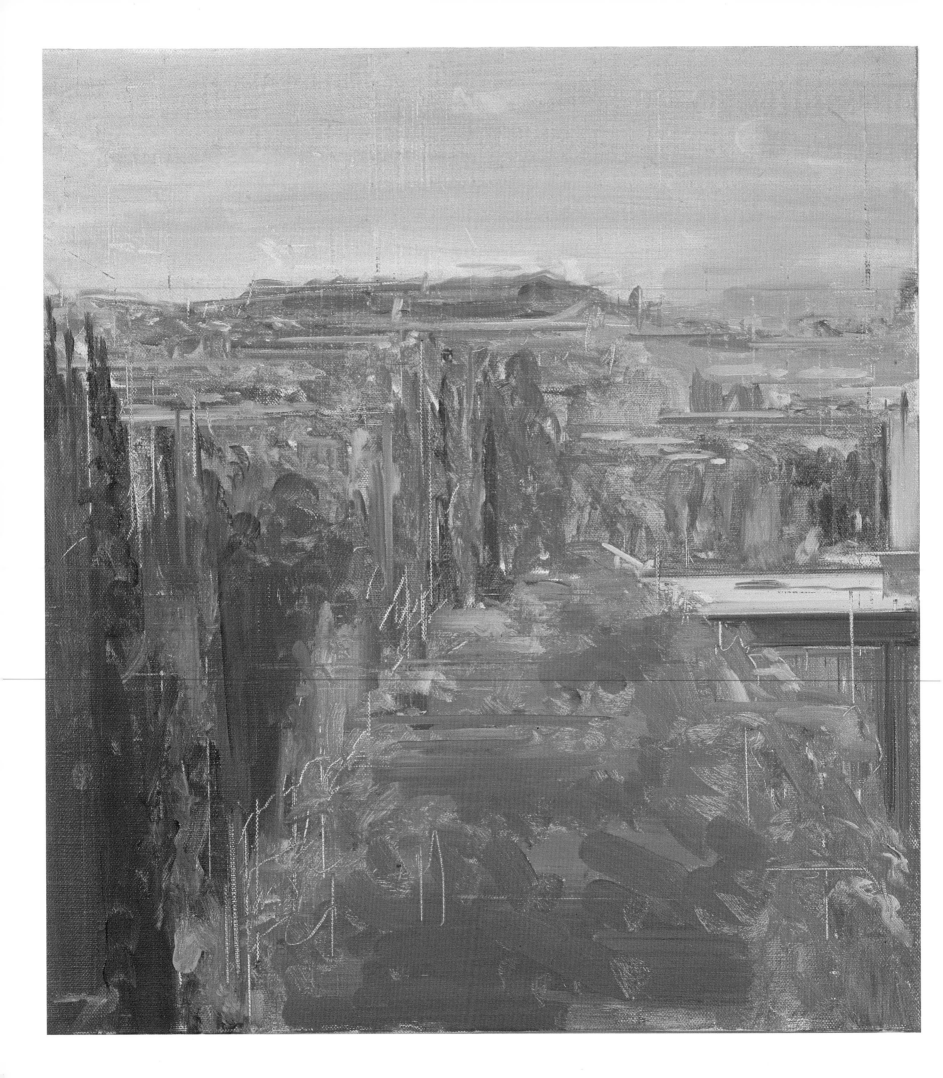

CHAPTER FIVE

On the days that I wasn't working to earn a living, I would sit in Café Peter from nine in the morning to three in the afternoon. If I was lucky, I might end up with only a single good page. To this day, I'm excited by a page of handwriting that doesn't need more work.

Not only émigrés from the Austro-Hungarian Empire frequented Café Peter, but there were also students, artists, lovers—all looking for a secluded place, and even generals with their secretaries. I would also come in sometimes with a girl. Ilana, the owner, would examine her from head to toe. If she didn't like her, I would be told. Once I brought in a beautiful and flamboyant young woman. Ilana looked her up and down. The next day she said to me, "You'll need eyes in the back of your head to hold on to that one. She's got hungry eyes, and she won't be satisfied with one man."

Ilana knew what she was talking about. Her acute senses would size people up, and I saw later the extent to which she was right.

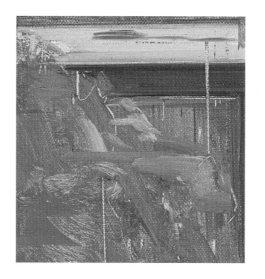

I would set out on my walks from Café Peter; I had a few regular trails. If I managed to write a clean page that I considered satisfactory, I would reward myself by setting out on foot to a place that I loved. One of them was the home of my friend Leib Rochman. He was a Yiddish writer whose book, *By Your Blood Will You Live,* was well known in Yiddish circles after the war. His home was a gathering place for Yiddish writers from all over the world. There, I met H. Leivick,

Haim Grade, Jacob Glatstein, A. Glanz-Leyeles—among many others. Yiddish literature in those years was already in decline, but it flourished at Rochman's home. Yiddish prose and poetry would be read in his living room late into the night, but mainly we sang and sang until we were drunk with the melodies. Rochman had the fiery enthusiasm of a hasidic rabbi. When my first book, *Smoke,* appeared, he embraced me and talked for almost an hour, praising my work. He knew that I was given to mood swings, that I was self-critical and painstaking. Even a minor success, instead of uplifting me, depresses me. He spoke in praise of my book, not in general terms, as people usually do, but by choosing passages and showing me what was good in them and what was new.

Survivors of the Holocaust, who should really have been my natural readers, did not read my book. In the 1950s and the 1960s most of them were busy trying to repress and forget the past and were fully immersed in building their new homes. They distanced themselves from my book as if from fire. And the survivors that did read it immediately found that what I was doing was not about bearing witness, but about giving life to my inner world. They were not happy with the way I did it—they were fanatic about bearing witness, and they considered anything that was not testimony distorted and false. I was happy that Rochman had liked my "fantasy."

My two first books were received with a certain understanding, but not enthusiasm. Leib Rochman read every story of mine and made his comments. He was like a volcano. Whatever he liked earned his exaggerated praise, and whatever he did not like was roundly and unsparingly criticized. His father had died when he was seven and he was brought up in the house of a hasidic rabbi and he had internalized hasidic thought in his home with his entire being. His judgments could be scathing. On more than one

CHAPTER SIX

occasion, he reviewed one of my short stories very harshly, but I always felt that he had immense love for me. He knew where I had come from, what I had been through, and he appreciated the progress I had made.

During the spring and summer, we would meet at Café Peter once a week and study a hasidic text together. Rochman had a quite extraordinary intuition for Jewish learning. He knew what was important, and what extraneous. He was not a scholar in the usual sense of the term, but he could read a page of the Talmud, or a portion of the Zohar, or a chapter of hasidic literature, with ease and great knowledge. I had come from an assimilated home that had a complicated relationship to Jewish life: in as far as it related to it at all, it related to its flaws. Rochman loved Jewish learning like one loves a woman, and it was this love that he passed on to me.

After the sessions with Rochman I would return to my room. I would walk to most places in Jerusalem. I loved the clear nights of spring. My studies at the university kept me busy, but they were far from all-absorbing; I was totally immersed in my writing. This was a passion that knew no bounds. Each new story was an effort to correct what had been flawed in the previous one. Till this very day I can sit for five or six hours, laboriously reworking and revising a page or two. Rewriting and editing do not tire me. After hours of such work, I feel like a farmer who has pulled up the weeds from his field.

O nce a week I would stroll around Rehavia at night. This was my neighborhood. During the 1950s and 1960s Rehavia had a life of its own. The low, well-tended houses reminded me of the quiet suburbs of the town of my birth. In summer the boarding houses were full of guests from the coastal plain. German was the main language in Rehavia and in the cafés. Because of the language and because of the well-tended houses, Rehavia did not look as if it belonged in new Israeli life. It carried far more resemblance to a residential neighborhood in Dresden, Leipzig, or Berlin. At Café Rehavia and Café Hermon you could get a cup of coffee and a piece of strudel that tasted just like the ones served in these cities. The conversations and the quiet tranquility were exactly like that of the small resort cities in the Carpathians, where we would travel every summer.

Here, the wretchedness of emigration was not to be seen. Those who sat in the cafés and in the gardens outside the houses did not look like uprooted people, but like those who had brought with them all their belongings from the land of their origin, so they could go on with their previous lives here.

These homes were closed to me. I was a poor student who earned his living from part-time work, and who dreamed of becoming a writer. But I would go to the neighborhood cafés, sit for hours and gaze at the people who surrounded me. The German spoken in Rehavia was not the German that I had heard at home. Here,

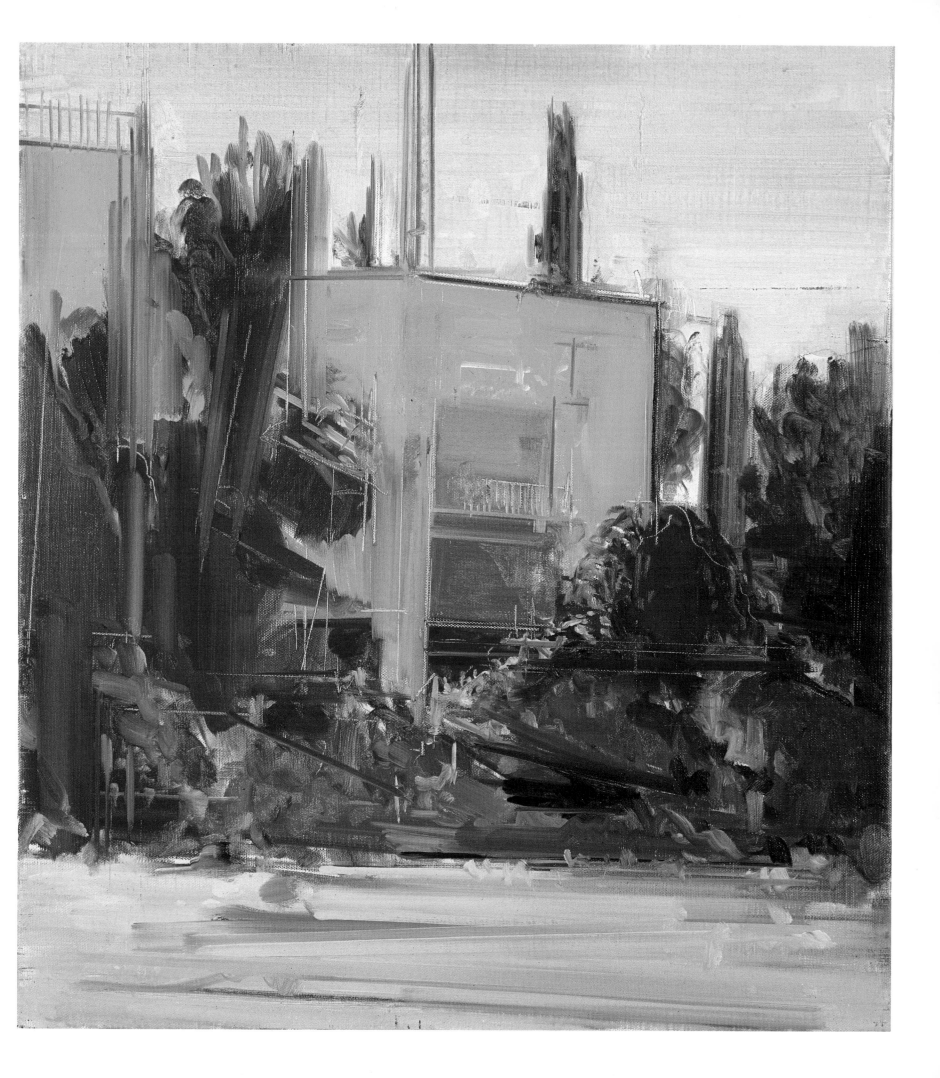

for some reason, it sounded more rigid. Words from Yiddish and from Slavic languages had crept into the German we had spoken in Czernowitz, softening it. Only much later, toward the end of the 1960s, did some homes belonging to this closed tribe open to me. In the 1950s, Rehavia and the university, which was then in the Terra Sancta building, were connected. Most of the teachers lived in Rehavia, and in the mornings you would see them hurrying to classes. It was on the steps of Terra Sancta that I saw Gershom Scholem for the first time—a man who was all eyes and ears.

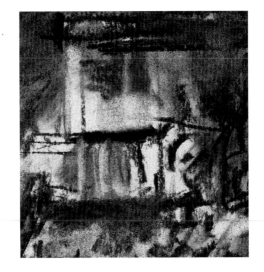

What from the outside appeared respectable, well tended and tranquil turned out, in fact, not to be so harmonious. During the 1950s and 1960s I took part—more as an observer— in several study groups held in private homes in the evenings. These study groups usually focused on a personality or a topic. One of the members of the group would prepare something to open up the discussion and the participants would respond.

The first study group that I took part in was on Kafka, the man and his work. Even at the very first meeting there was dissention: whether Kafka should be read as a Jewish author whose writing, beyond the complex personal issues, describes Jewish characters and Jewish fate—or whether he should be seen as universal. The majority in the study group saw Kafka as universal, a writer who spoke a language that transcended nationalities. Yet the contradictory facts had been gathered by Max Brod, Kafka's long-time friend. Brod, who was invited to the study group, argued that Kafka was a Jewish writer not only because his parents and his close friends were Jewish; and not only because he had deep yearnings toward Jewish creativity, a feeling for Yiddish, for poetry and theater in Yiddish, for the Hebrew language and for Jewish thinking, but beyond all this—he should be regarded as a Jewish writer because of the very essence of his work. After all, who was that person in *The Trial*, the person who stood accused, but had committed no crime—the person in the grip of anxiety, shunted back and forth between different courtrooms; who was this person, if not the persecuted Jew?

Two retired lawyers participated in these discussions, a retired judge, and some industrialists. I immediately saw that these respectable people approached the texts with understanding and sensitivity, but there was also hidden anger at their "Jewishness" for having brought so many catastrophes upon them. I was very familiar with assimilated Jews from home, but in contrast to the Jews of Germany, Bukovina's assimilated Jews seemed extremely Jewish. It wasn't that my own city of Czernowitz didn't also have a good number of self-hating Jews among the petit-bourgeoisie, but that self-hatred was already well established for many generations among the Jews of Germany.

After an hour and a half of discussion, the hostess would serve tea and cakes. My landlady, at whose home the study group took place, was a librarian by profession. In Israel, however, because she didn't speak the language, she didn't work. She would rent out two rooms to two students. For years she had tried to learn Hebrew, the students who had been there before me had also tried to teach her, but though she spoke French, English, and Italian, to say nothing of German, she found it hard to put together a simple sentence in Hebrew.

When she heard that I was studying Yiddish at the university, she was astonished and said: "Why? Whatever for? You already speak German, English and Russian—who needs this language?!"

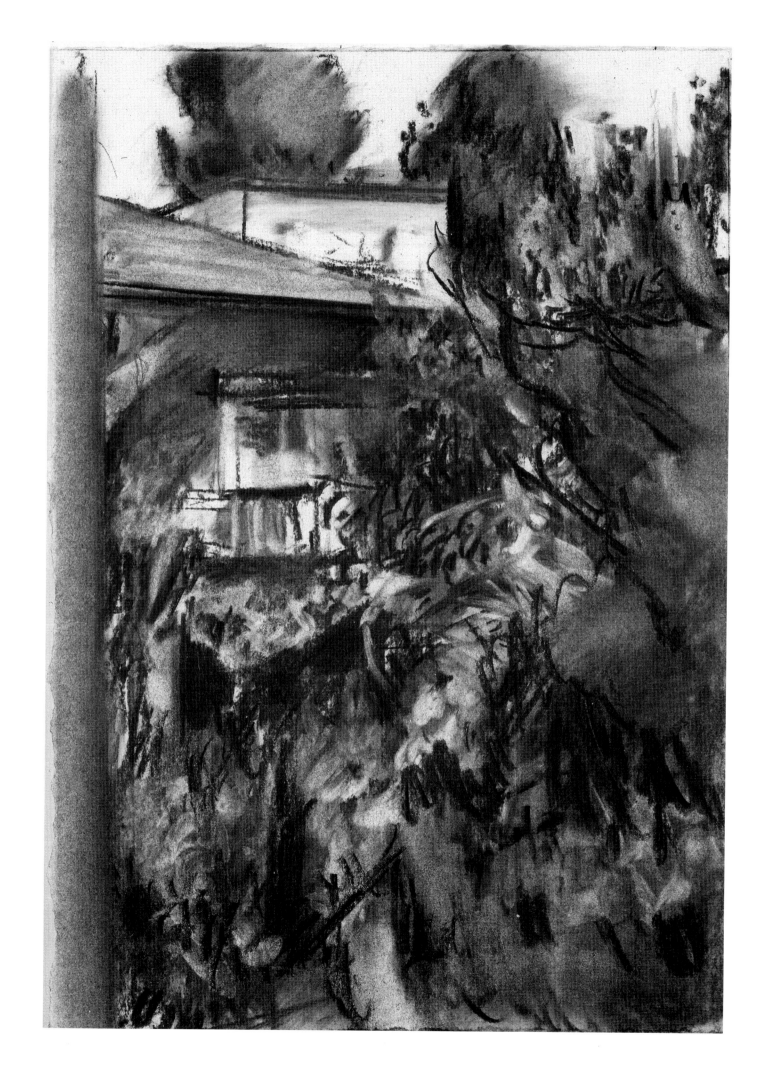

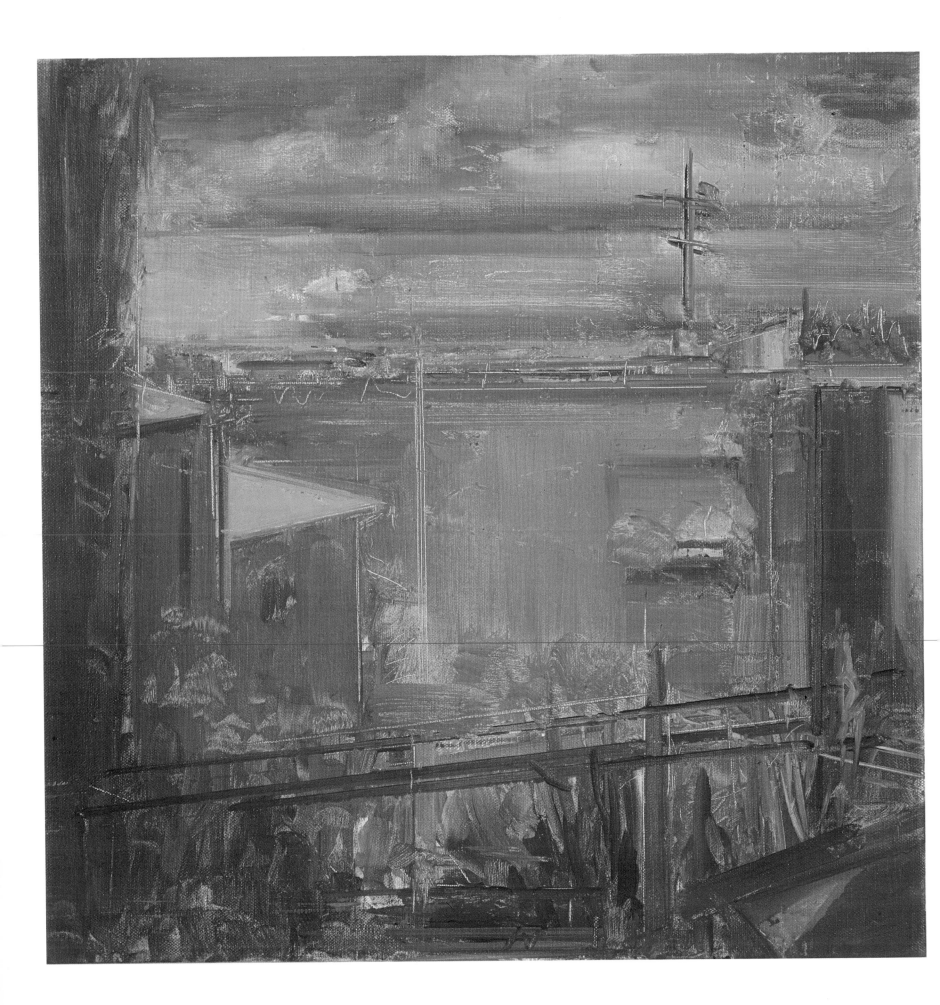

All the prejudices that she had harbored for years came out in this short exchange. From time to time she would remind me that I should study a profession that would enlarge my knowledge and be useful. Though sensitive to the sufferings of others and a regular volunteer at the Bikur Holim Hospital, she could find not one compassionate word to say about the language of the Jews. Once she didn't restrain herself and exclaimed, "The catastrophe of the Jews is all due to Yiddish!"

It was at her home that I saw what assimilation had done to the Jewish soul. Even the most ghastly terrors of the Holocaust had not managed to uproot the yearning of Jews for the country where they were born.

As early as the 1950s, several couples had left Rehavia to go back to live in Germany. These educated and sensitive people, who appreciated good music, read texts with great sensitivity and gave lucid expression to their thoughts, were at a loss when it came to their Jewishness. For the majority of them, their "Jewishness" was a burden. But for me, Rehavia became the threshold to my home, from which I had been uprooted in childhood. Here, everything resembled my hometown—the leafy boulevards, the courtyards, the quiet, the small well-tended stores; toward nightfall, flowing from the open windows, the strains of a piano or a violin. The years in the Youth Aliyah and in the army had erased many dear memories. Walking around the streets of Rehavia brought back to me the taste of shady streets, of the blossoming of acacia and lilac. And in this way, quite imperceptibly, I was given back a tiny part of the vast loss.

CHAPTER SEVEN

From Café Peter I would set out once a month for the youth farm next to Armon Hanatziv, on the outskirts of Jerusalem. I had arrived there with a group of children in 1946. It was my start in the country.

The farm was situated on a hill, overlooking magical vistas on two sides. From the east side, the bleached Judean hills, and far from them, the mountains of Moab, which toward evening would be enveloped in swathes of blue mist. To the west—the old City, which from far off looked like a rocky outcrop, with the golden dome glistening on the top of its skull. Toward evening the skies would open and light would be poured from them.

After years of rain and snow, I felt as if I had emerged from a tunnel toward the light. I loved the light. Within a short time, I had found several observation points and would spend hours gazing from them, sometimes till nightfall. But the nights were not magical. When I slept, I was still *there*, wandering and hiding myself or running, at my last gasp. Sometimes I would awaken amid shouts. I was not the only one. There were other children who would shout in their sleep and awaken.

Life on the youth farm was intense: four hours of learning Hebrew and Bible, and four hours of manual labor. In the evening, exhaustion would descend on me, weighing down on my eyelids, but I strained not to enter the world of shadows, and I would sit and read for hours.

There were days when it would seem to me that the strength of the ghosts was weakening and that soon they would leave me alone, and there were signs of this. But at the time I did not know that it was my fate to live in two worlds. Then it still seemed to me

The two years at the youth farm were a tangle of groping with the new place, while struggling with oblivion, nightmares, the agonies of sex and the feeling that my body, despite everything, was growing stronger. It was at the youth farm that I learned how to build terraces, to plant saplings on them and to take care of the fruit trees that were planted. There were days when I suffered from sunburn, from fatigue, but on fair or partially cloudy days, I felt that I was growing and changing, connecting somehow with the fruit trees that I was planting. My dream at that time was to become a farmer and to have my own horse and plow.

that the lofty skies, working the earth, the heroes from the Book of Judges, who we were learning about in class—that they would all bring about the miracle, they would uproot us from the "there", and would plant us within these hills.

Rachel Yanait (Ben-Zvi), the director of the farm, was an impressive woman, a commander type. From my very first days at the youth farm she had noticed that I read—I had been immersed in some old geography book in German, which I had found in the Atlit detention camp. "What are you reading, and in what language?" The inevitable questions. I told her. "You should be reading in Hebrew," she said decisively.

I didn't respond. During the war I learned not to ask and not to respond, but to listen and to follow. These traits, which I acquired then, have stayed with me to this very day.

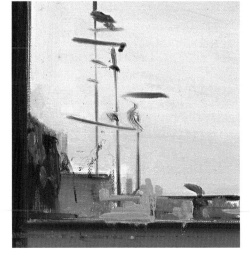

In the evening, I would return to my workplace in the nursery, to check whether the grafting had taken, and if the seedlings I had planted had taken root. The earth and the seedlings brought me happiness. I would sit for hours and gaze at the blue hills of Moab and secretly rejoice in my solitude. During these wonderful hours, far from my friends, I would jot things down in a notebook.

Rachel Yanait caught me reading at night in one of the empty classrooms.
"What are you reading?" she pressed me, repeatedly.
I told her.
Again, she made her predictable comments.
Of course, I didn't answer her.

Then she told me that she wanted to have a long talk with me. Her warning made me anxious, sowing disquiet. But I need not have worried, for the talk never took place. In the spring of 1948 our situation deteriorated. The youth farm was under siege, being fired upon from all sides. Work and studies ceased, and everyone was enlisted to defend this isolated place. At first we practiced with sticks, and then later, they brought in some Sten guns. I was also chosen to use an automatic gun, and my delight knew no bounds.

Even at home, I had loved leafing through books and reading what I could. Then, at the British detention camp at Atlit, south of Haifa, when I came across any books in German, I'd read them. The thought that I could read and understand what was written made me so happy that I didn't put the books down for a moment.

In Atlit the sun burned fiercely and the salt seared us. Our skin was covered with burns and blisters. But I read thirstily, as if quarrying out a cave for myself. At the youth farm too, I continued to devour books at the same rate. To my surprise, I found some German novels in one of the storerooms. Rachel Yanait knew about this and whenever she saw me reading, she would ask, "What are you reading?"

She said whatever she said, and I, for my part, did my utmost to keep out of her sight.

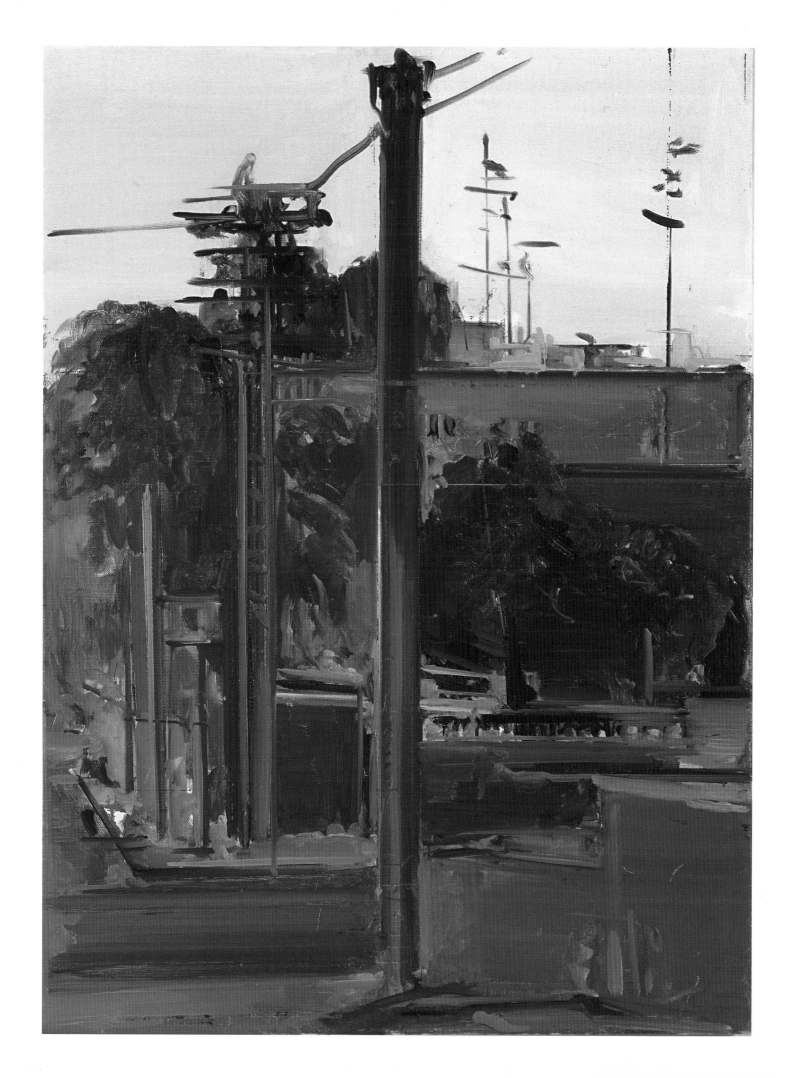

CHAPTER EIGHT

Then, of course, we did not know that we were so few, pitted against a huge incited mob. The instructors and the students took up various positions to defend the place. We had no chance. Every night, a hail of gunfire would rain down on us. When the siege intensified, we retreated under the cover of darkness from the youth farm toward the city.

Since then some fifty years have passed. Sometimes it seems to me that I'm still standing there, stirred by the immense light, building a terrace or digging ditches, or dreaming of joining the army and serving in the Palmach.

Many years later Rachel Yanait would say, "You were an introverted child, you didn't join in, and you read books in German."

I was already a well-known Hebrew author, but she hadn't forgotten my sins.

From the start of the 1950s, until it closed, I would frequent Café Rehavia on Ramban Street. The place reminded me of cafés in the resort towns that we used to travel to each summer. Unlike Café Peter, here all the conversations were in German. You saw at once that these refugees had not been in a ghetto; they had not been in railway stations crowded with people and packages, nor in a concentration camp. The comfort and ease of the places they had come from still clung to them.

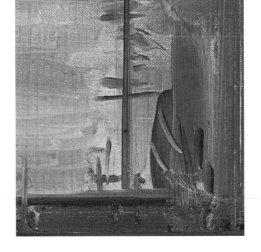

I once saw a man sitting there playing chess against himself. I suggested playing with him and he agreed. He played a tough, decisive game, each move was well thought out and carefully considered. I was also careful, but only up to a certain point; then my patience would run out, and of course I'd lose.

That's how we became friends and I acquired a chess partner. His name was Manfred Zauber. He was about fifty, tall and slim, and unlike most of the people who came to this café, simply dressed.

"Where are you from?" he found the courage to ask after several meetings. I told him.
"What do you want to do after you finish your studies?"
I told him.

Even then, the torment of writing was not unfamiliar to me. I might work at a page for hours, tear it up, and then go back to

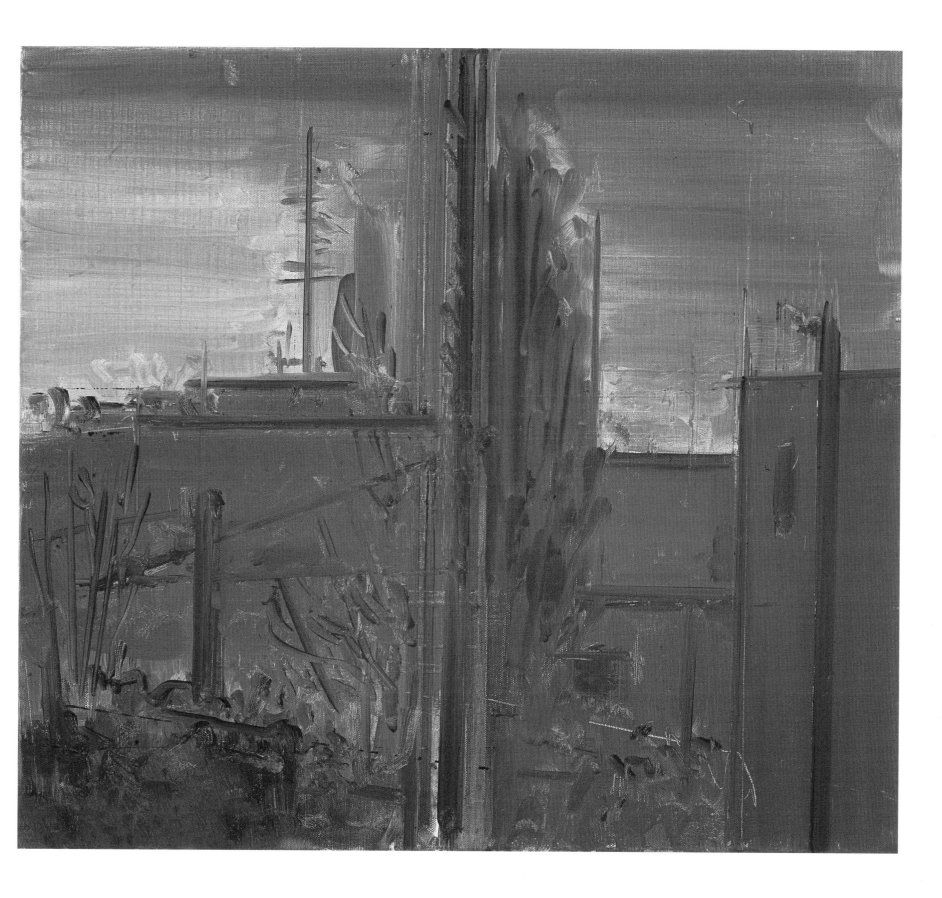

writing it all over again. Kafka and Agnon were the authors that I loved, but I couldn't follow in their path.

I loved playing with Zauber. His extreme cautiousness spurred me to take risks and make ever more imaginative moves. I loved his astonishment at the sight of one of my daring moves. In Hannover, the city where he was born, he had been the Registrar at the Hannover law courts. Perhaps because of his height and his long, gaunt body, he reminded me of Kafka. It turned out that I was not the only one who had noticed the resemblance; others saw it as well. It amused Zauber. Once I saw his wife. She seemed to be a female replica, cut to his proportions, tall and slender. They did not have children.

Zauber completely changed my relationship to Café Rehavia. Up to the time I met him, I had focused on only the distorted or even grotesque aspects of these lucky people who had fled Nazi Germany in time. Now I was faced with a man who, before each game, would stick a cigarette in a holder, light it with a lighter, stretch out his long arm and move one of the pieces. The tremor of hesitation always accompanied any movement of his hand. He was a very closed person who scarcely uttered a word.

Once he surprised me by asking me if I had read Kleist.
"No."
"An important writer, I'll lend you his books."

As soon as I started to read them I understood: this was a writer from whom I could learn. Throughout the 1950s, I had written short stories, but wasn't happy with them. It was clear to me that I knew neither the secret of plot development nor the power of simply stated facts. Instead of searching for a correct fact, I reach for metaphors. An excess of metaphors produces an unpleasant mist and a false sense of the poetic. The right facts, one following the next, are the driving force, the engine that moves a story along. A story, like a river, cannot stand still in one place.

I told Zauber my impressions and he agreed with me. He added: "In Kleist you can see the flame of justice." No sooner had he said these words, then the person in front of me was no longer Zauber, the refugee who had ended up in Rehavia, but the Registrar of the Hannover Court of Law, who for years had maintained the great order and high moral standards of his office, but who had eventually been forced to flee in haste with the forged papers that his cousin had somehow secured for him.

Jerusalem cafés not only brought me close to people to whom I sought to be close, but also to some kind of principle, some core. I had never liked abstractions, but as with most people, I got enmeshed in them. Among other things, being in cafés taught me about the affinity that exists between the extremely private and the general. There were times when I let my writing sink into details, believing that a plethora of detail would bring out an important principle. Naturally, I was mistaken.

The sights that I absorbed in Café Rehavia sometimes served as a platform and background for my novels, such as *Badenheim 1939*, or *The Age of Wonders*. As for Zauber himself—I have not yet written about him, but his name has crept into some of my stories.

Once I saw Gershom Scholem striding determinedly into Café Rehavia. Completely enraged, he looked like he was about to give someone there a piece of his mind. But when I came in, I found him sitting alone, reading a newspaper and sipping coffee.

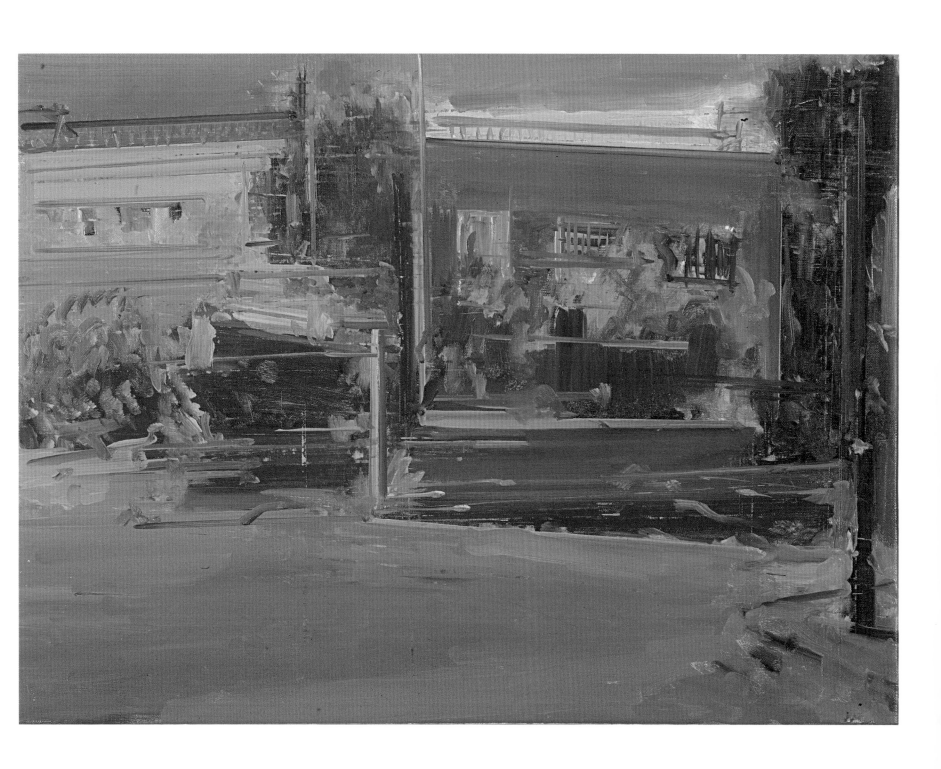

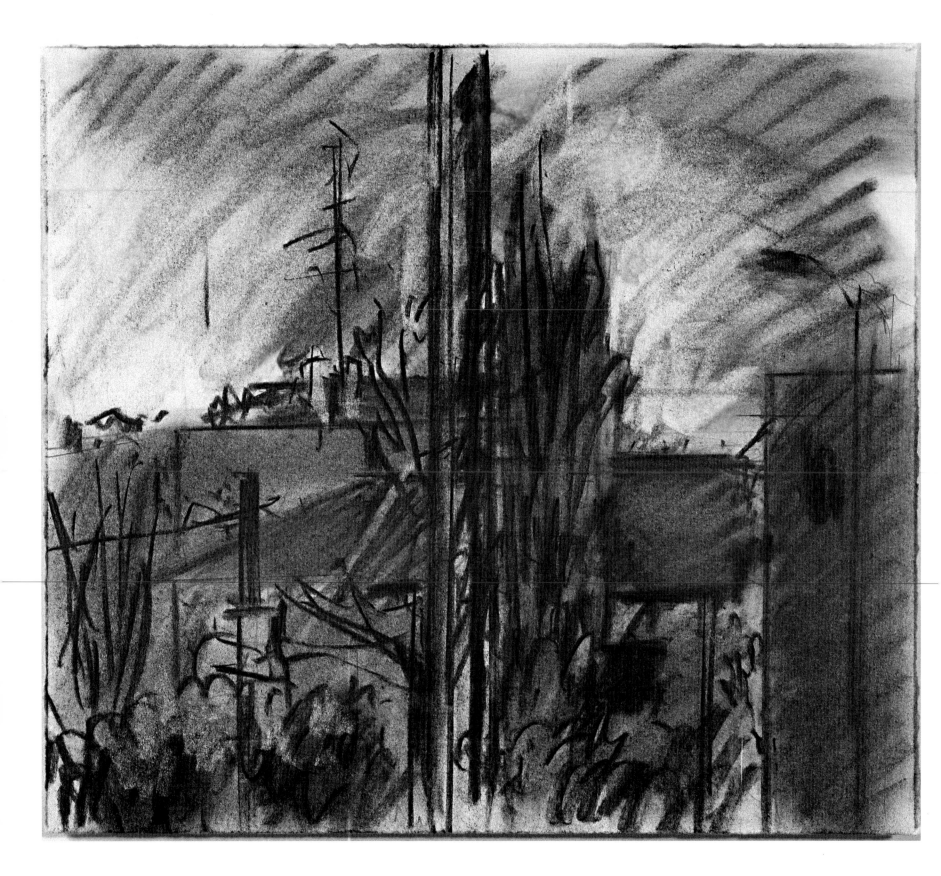

CHAPTER NINE

The 1950s and 1960s were witness to two wars, but there wasn't really a lull even between them. During the Sinai Campaign I was assigned to a team positioned at Upper Motza, outside Jerusalem. The Jordanian army, which was supposed to attack us, did not attack. For days on end, we would lie around next to the mortars. From time to time we might move around, stir ourselves and exercise, but most days passed without doing anything. We lived off canned food and cigarettes, which dulled our thoughts. I had brought a few books with me but never touched them. At that time, seen from the heights of Motza, life seemed utterly purposeless. Little by little, anxiety receded, leaving only a sense of emptiness. No wonder that soldiers squabbled over the most trivial things. One soldier who couldn't take this long drawn-out waiting period actually deserted.

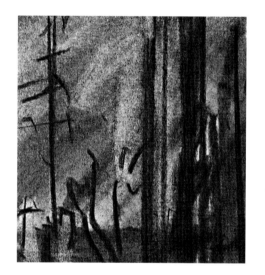

A month of being cut off from my reading, from my notebooks and writing, and from myself, left me adrift. At the end of the war, I felt that I should be more involved in daily events, to note things down on a daily basis so that at some point I would be able to understand the driving force behind life's complexity, and how it works. Yet it was fortunate that I wasn't drawn into this "encompassing" idea. Literature cannot compete with the great flow of life. Literature is basically a sideways glance, loyal to a specific cross-section of life. It doesn't cut you off from other parts of life, nor is it a way of secluding yourself; but it certainly isn't "everything". In the end, "everything" is as good as nothing.

Several people tried to dissuade me from this path. Newspapers proposed that I write a weekly column and some institutions suggested that I write profiles of well-known figures. These temptations were supposed to help me make a living. Instinct told me not to follow that path.

I'm not so sure if my stubborn loyalty to my writing has always served me well. But at any rate, following my instincts didn't fail me. Instead, I was involved with people whose interior lives resembled my own. For the most part they were people wounded in their childhood, and their wound is the radar through which they take in the world. I believed, and still believe, that people who went through the Holocaust have thoughts and feelings that can contribute to the understanding of others. The experiences that we went through taught us not only about human weakness, but also about the nobility of man. It was these truths that I needed to learn by simply listening to myself, while at the same time trying to ignore official commentators: newspapers, radio, the university, to say nothing of political wrangling. What I needed in those years was a breathing space of my own, a space where I could have a relationship with myself and people who had experienced what I had experienced. The café was the place that suited me. In a café you can see uncensored movement, body language. Sometimes the entire war might be expressed with a shrug of the shoulder.

For years, I observed Tina and Arthur from close at Café Peter. I would eagerly await their arrival, and grew anxious if they were late. I never talked to them, and they did not address me, as if it were understood that our friendship would always be from a distance. Even though they were years older than me, we were so alike. However, they were more open, and could express their inner world better than I could. More than anything, what I most appreciated and respected in them and their friends, was their way

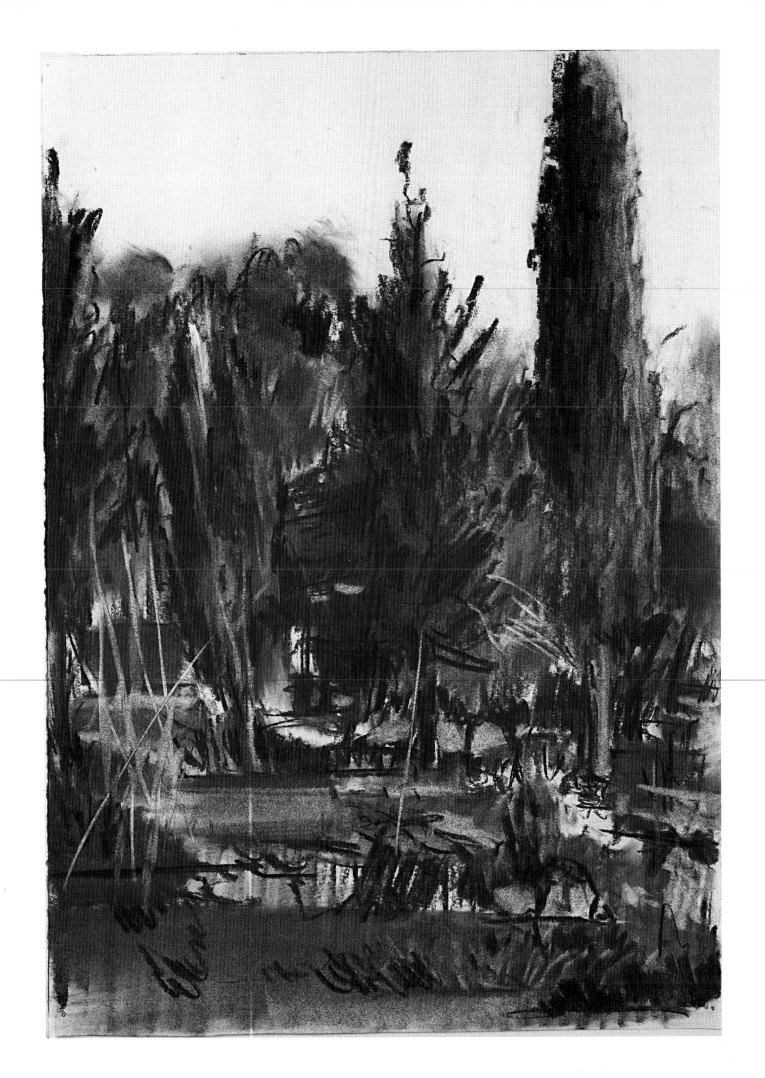

confronting the world—their very being spoke of understand-
g through silence.

te and suffering had kneaded their flesh, putting Tina in a
heelchair; and as for Big Arthur, he had been violently robbed
his large family. Arthur, who could have easily earned a living
d loved his extended family, had been left alone in life. This
g man would sit for hours without uttering a word. Sometimes
seemed as if he were about to jump up from his chair and say
mething shocking. But this was not in Arthur's nature. He was
ways enveloped in his silence. He raised silence to the level of
ayer. Sometimes it seemed that he was about to fall on his knees
d cross himself, like the sturdy peasants from my region.

was at Café Peter that I heard people say, "Don't ask. What is
ere to say? I don't like it when they talk about it. Why talk about
?" That's how they kept circling the great disasters of their lives
d in this way, they also taught me how to live in silence.

CHAPTER TEN

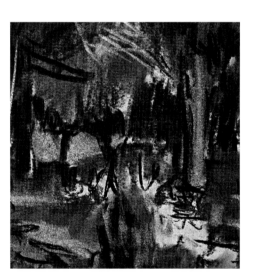

I would go to Café Rehavia once or twice a week, mainly
during the afternoon, and play a game or two with Zauber.
Sometimes his decisive game would drive me crazy. I would
embark on an adventure, and lose of course. Sometimes
it seemed that Zauber was so immersed in
himself that outside things didn't affect him.
At other times he would surprise me and tell
me something about the city of his birth. But
he never spoke about his former position,
which had been a high one. Once he revealed
to me that many years ago he had thought of
joining a kibbutz, but nothing had come of it.
This refined man did not love religious Jews.
When I told him that I would occasionally
go to the religious neighborhood of Sha'arei
Hesed, he made a gesture of revulsion.

Not far from Café Rehavia, on Keren Kayemet
Street, was the Hermon coffee house, an open-
air café with a long garden. At Café Hermon there were fewer
intimate areas than at Café Rehavia, but despite this, it stimulated
my writing. Sometimes a crowded place and terrible coffee get the
prose flowing, whereas a quiet place, though well kept and clean,
can block my writing and weigh on my spirit. At Café Hermon I
didn't write a lot, but what I wrote became part of my books.

From Café Hermon, I would set out on an occasional stroll around
Sha'arei Hesed and Nachlaot, or walk down to the Valley of the
Cross. In the 1950s and 1960s there were open spaces at the edge
of each neighborhood. On several occasions, after failing to write
anything, I would abandon my table and leave the café, and go
out for a walk. Sometimes this stroll would loosen up an impasse

in my writing, and sometimes it put the right words into my pen. Once I entered one of the little synagogues in Sha'arei Hesed. An old Jewish man came up to me, and without asking me anything, laid his palms on my head and blessed me. Sometimes, after three or four hours of writing, I might produce a few good paragraphs and then I would immediately take a stroll. A leisurely walk after some productive efforts is a sheer delight.

At Café Hermon I would meet up with Shlomo Zemach, Immanuel Olsvanger, and Yitzhak Shenhar. Sometimes Yehoshua Tan-Pai would wander in. Shlomo Zemach had a reputation for being a harsh and intransigent critic. I loved his pithy observations. His general education and his Jewish knowledge were both wide-ranging and he was always ready

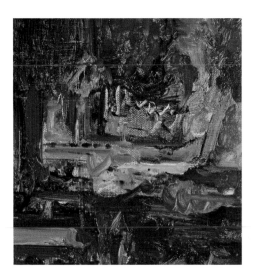

with an apt definition, a wise sentence on a novel or some work of criticism. His book, *About Beauty*, is among the cornerstones of aesthetic thought in Hebrew. Zemach was a critic who introduced new concepts, values and well-structured thinking into the loose impressionism of Hebrew criticism. His articles were all highly crafted. No less than the critic, I loved Shlomo Zemach of the Second Aliyah, an agronomist, the director of the Kadouri Agricultural school, a childhood friend of David Ben-Gurion. An hour with Shlomo Zemach was invariably inspiring and broadened my horizons.

Sometimes I would visit Shlomo Zemach together with Leib Rochman in Zemach's house on Gaza Street. Rochman and Zemach were both born in Poland, and they had a common language. During these evening conversations at Zemach's home, they would bring alive the spirit of Polish Jewry: what there had been and what had been lost. Zemach liked us because he saw us as witnesses to the Jewish world that had been destroyed. He

would embarrass us by saying that he had great respect for those survivors who had not lost their humanity.

The writer Yitzhak Shenhar kept trying to get me to change my name and do some translating work. He claimed that the craft of translation helps an author, particularly translating from classic literature. When he found out that I was born in Czernowitz, he was convinced that I must be proficient in German. Instinct told me, however, that it was best for me to distance myself from this kind of work. Naturally, a writer has to learn and study, but he shouldn't develop at the expense of great writers. He has to be what he is. At one point I gave him my first book *Smoke*. He summarized his impressions in a terse sentence: "Your Hebrew is still young."

When I read Shenhar's own prose and his translations, I understood that for him language was a supreme value.

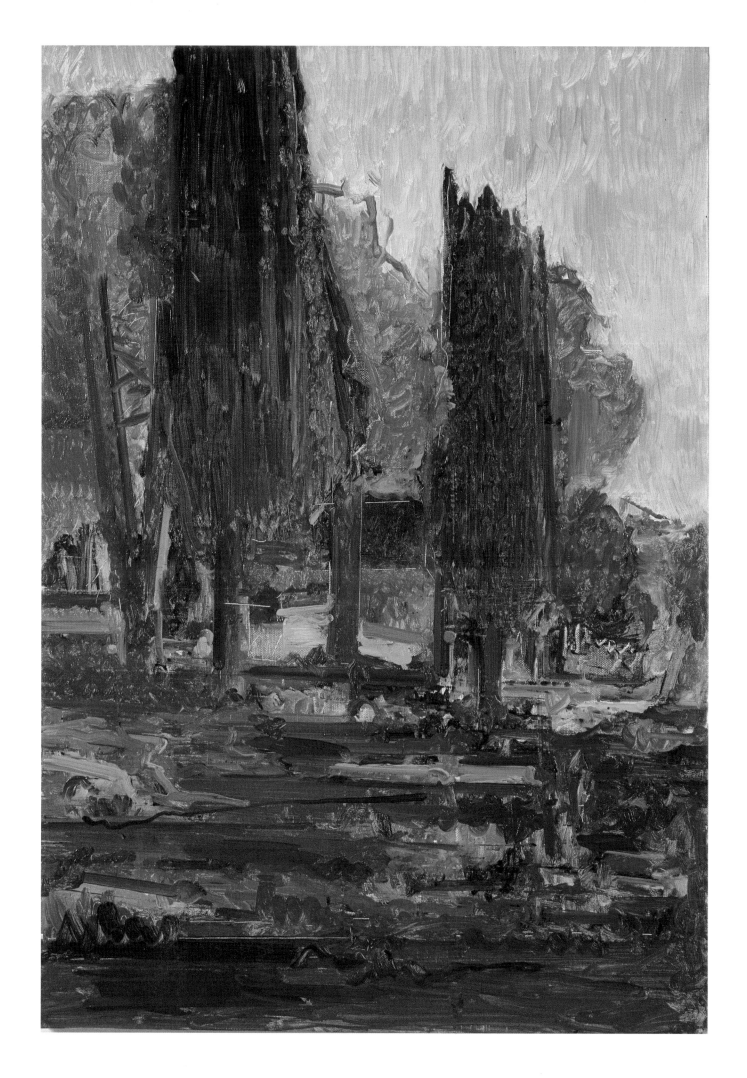

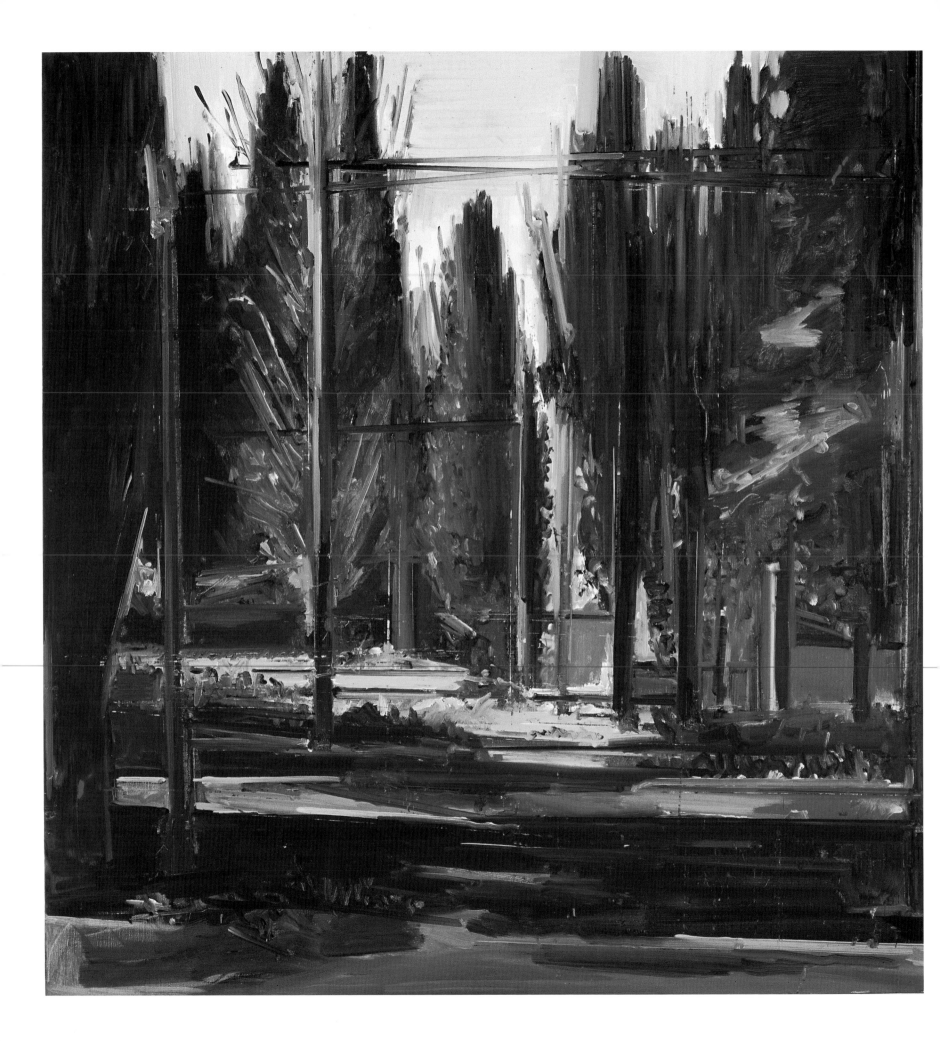

CHAPTER ELEVEN

If I ever stayed away from Café Peter for a day or two, I would slink back as if I were guilty. Ilana, the proprietress, suspected that I had been deceiving her. Naturally, I denied it, and claimed that if I went to other cafés, it was never at the expense of Café Peter. It was my beloved place; nothing could replace it.

It really was how I felt, and it was only at Café Peter that I could write steadily for hours on end. It was there that I was relieved of the constraints of the short story and started to write novels. Café Peter had everything I needed: good coffee, a glass of cognac, and a cigarette. These three-fold drugs kept me going for years, but even more than this, I was enchanted by the people who surrounded me and saw myself reflected in their loneliness.

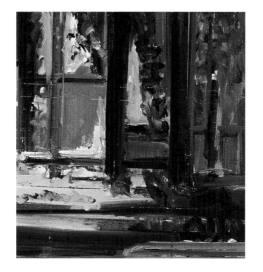

Tina would appear at the café entrance like a princess. Despite her severe disability, she never relinquished a drop of her dignity. In her last years she suffered from high blood pressure and diabetes. The doctors gave her a special diet, and though she kept to it, from time to time she would declare, "A piece of cheesecake today—and never mind the consequences!"

Her friends would occasionally move her from her wheelchair to a padded wicker chair. This must have been very painful, but Tina never complained. Once, after they had transferred her from chair to chair, I heard her joking: "I'm not bound to a man, but bound to this wheelchair."

There was nobility in everything Tina did. In the years I had wandered the roads, been in hiding places and transit camps, I had seen much ugliness and suffering. I was thirsty for something spiritual, for nobility. Tina imbued her surroundings with a freedom and beauty that came from within. It was no wonder that the young women that I dated at the time seemed to me lacking and soulless.

The high point of my week was meeting Leib Rochman. At Café Peter we read many mystical hasidic texts. The way Rochman studied was far from systematic. His was a stormy spirit, extremely associative, but he always alighted upon some central truth. Reading with him brought me closer to Hasidism than did Martin Buber's *Light of the Hidden*. Buber's book opened the first gate before me. The works of original, unpolished Hasidism that we read were a blend brimming with intense faith, folk tales, and sudden flashes. In other words, religion in all its spiritual and earthly components. Buber wiped off the dust from hasidic learning so that modern Jews would be able to appreciate it without being ashamed of it. With Rochman, I read Hasidism as it was.

After my first book was published, journalists came to interview me. Their first question was: "When are you going to start writing about Israel?" At first I would apologize, telling them a little about my life. They weren't satisfied with that, they demanded a promise. Instead of making me happy, I found these interviews somewhat embarrassing. I felt I was engaged in something significant, but the spokesmen for culture in Israel thought otherwise. No wonder I started to question what I was doing. My book, *Smoke,* (1962) had dealt with war and with immigration—issues that have always characterized Israel. There were immigrants everywhere. Without anyone noticing, they changed the face of every street and neighborhood. By raising the immigrant from an anonymous individual to that of a suffering man, I was in the avant-garde, allowing readers to experience immigrants as sensitive people, whose feelings

CHAPTER TWELVE

and thoughts may be contradictory, but who were also alive and active within their inner landscape. In the immigrant I found everything that there was in me. Disquiet, feelings of inferiority, guilt. However, there was not only weakness to be found in all of us, but also the ability to adapt and renew ourselves. The immigrant is not a nameless individual; he carries deep within him worlds that are wrapped in pain and suffering. I tried to remove the layers encasing him, to reveal the beauty within the pain.

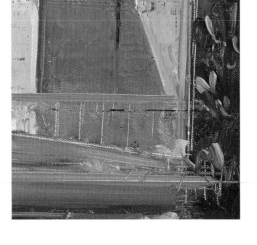

During these years, Professor Shimon Halkin would speak about the "uprooted." But someone who has survived the Holocaust has not been uprooted in the social sense. He has been through hell, and the fires of hell cling to his skin. One can speak about deep social anguish, and even about anguish of the soul—but what is there to say about hell? Wandering around in Israel at that time were thousands of survivors with open wounds. To speak in outdated, pre-Second World War terms about these people's scars would have been to desecrate their pain.

Lea Goldberg was among the few to take note of my short stories. She was my teacher at the university, and her opinion was important to me. Referring to one of the reviews that criticized my work, she said, "Don't take any notice, it comes from a lack of understanding—and vulgarity too."

She herself had written a play about the Holocaust, but in her heart of hearts she knew that what she had written about the Holocaust was not exactly "Holocaust" and did not penetrate the essence of the tragedy. Once she told me, "Only Dante, one of the great geniuses of all time, was able to write about hell."

I loved her simplicity. She was never artificial and never pretended. Neither was there any discrepancy between her appearance and what she said. What painful honesty.

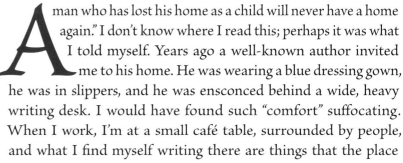

A man who has lost his home as a child will never have a home again." I don't know where I read this; perhaps it was what I told myself. Years ago a well-known author invited me to his home. He was wearing a blue dressing gown, he was in slippers, and he was ensconced behind a wide, heavy writing desk. I would have found such "comfort" suffocating. When I work, I'm at a small café table, surrounded by people, and what I find myself writing there are things that the place evokes in me. Every place gives you its own words, its rhythm. At a café I'm at the center of an arena, battling. Sometimes I manage to overcome the chaos and I put together a paragraph or two, but mostly I'm defeated.

The thing to do after sitting in a café is to take a walk. A walk is also a way to reach what's hidden in yourself, as it brings you closer to your surroundings and the landscape. When I walk around, I'm not in search of a new place. I'm always returning to the same places and I'm happy to meet someone there whom I already know. The coming back, even more than setting out, is what opens my eyes. I can return to the same place year after year and still be surprised by the small changes.

Some years ago, in America, I met a writer well known for his travel books. Every year he goes off to a different country and every year or two there's a new book of his on the market. I wonder what he could have taken in during these hasty visits, what his eye might have absorbed.

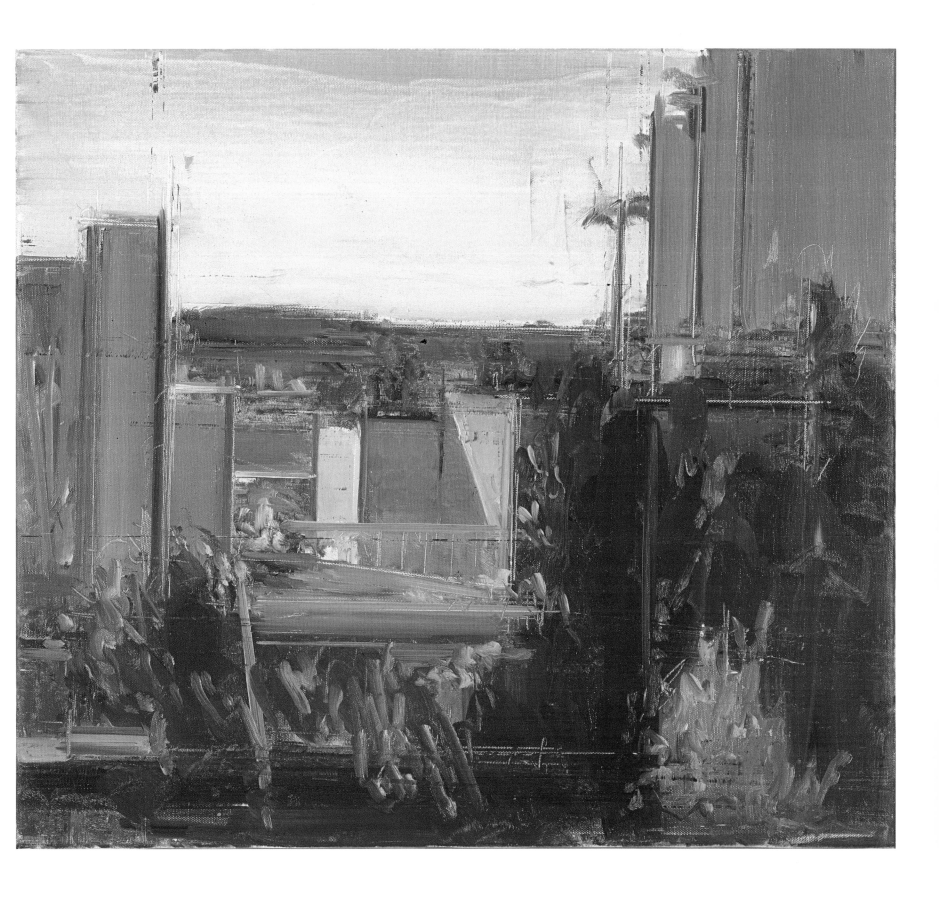

In this, as in other ways, Agnon and I spoke the same language. Agnon's world had its roots in local surroundings, which provided him with a foothold and an anchor through all his wanderings. Agnon also loved to go for walks; like me, he too liked going back to the same places, where the small details would always catch his eye. Once he stood looking at a cat. It seemed to me that he was staring at its shape and the color of its fur. To my surprise, he said to me, "Don't you think that cats, more than any other animal, are the incarnation of a soul?" And then he added, "Writers of the Enlightenment had no understanding of the mysteries of life. Neither do writers in our day."

Agnon had two cities, Buczacz and Jerusalem, but in his writing they got reversed: Buczacz was spiritual and imaginary, while Jerusalem was real and tangible. He would leave no stone unturned in Meah Shearim, but he also knew Rehavia well and knew which architects had built the more impressive houses in the neighborhood.

Agnon, who was finely attuned to human weakness, took me to task on the way I would use cafés, and he would claim that "holiness does not dwell in a café." Once he caught sight of a woman researcher, whose field was Hasidism, sitting in a crowded café, totally immersed in a book by one of the masters. He couldn't contain himself, and went over to her and gave her a piece of his mind.

My strolls with Leib Rochman in Meah Shearim, which were mostly at night, were different. Rochman was not as thorough as Agnon, but his enthusiasm compensated for this weakness. Hasidism was in his soul, and he knew it inside out; he was sensitive to the slightest rustle in Meah Shearim at night. He knew, for example, in which synagogues coffee was drunk and in which tea—and why. He even knew why a particular text would be studied at certain hours of the night. Here in Meah Shearim, the customs that had been prevalent in small towns in Poland and in Galicia, were kept to the absolute letter. On more than one occasion we

would enter a synagogue where people were studying Torah, sit down and listen to the sing-song melodies of learning, or we might even join. The thought that the Jews of Meah Shearim—they and their parents before them, who had already been born in the neighborhood—not only remembered, but were actively keeping up the customs of their forefathers who had lived at a distance of thousands of miles from here, this was a thought that always moved Rochman deeply.

For me, these walks were like entering my hidden consciousness. It was here that I connected with my grandparents and here that they passed on to me what they hadn't managed to pass on during their lifetime. On more than one occasion Rochman would exclaim, "What other people has a history that is actually lived today by living people?! We really have to cherish these people at all costs! Everyone should come here and find out to what branch of Hasidism his forefathers belonged and learn as much as they can from them."

Whenever he would discover a prayer melody or whenever he heard of a new custom, he would be as delighted as a child. He considered melodies and customs no less important than religious law. Though outwardly secular, Rochman would change when he was in Meah Shearim. It were as if his forefathers and their ancestors had become part of him. No wonder that the Jews of Meah Shearim treated him as one of their own.

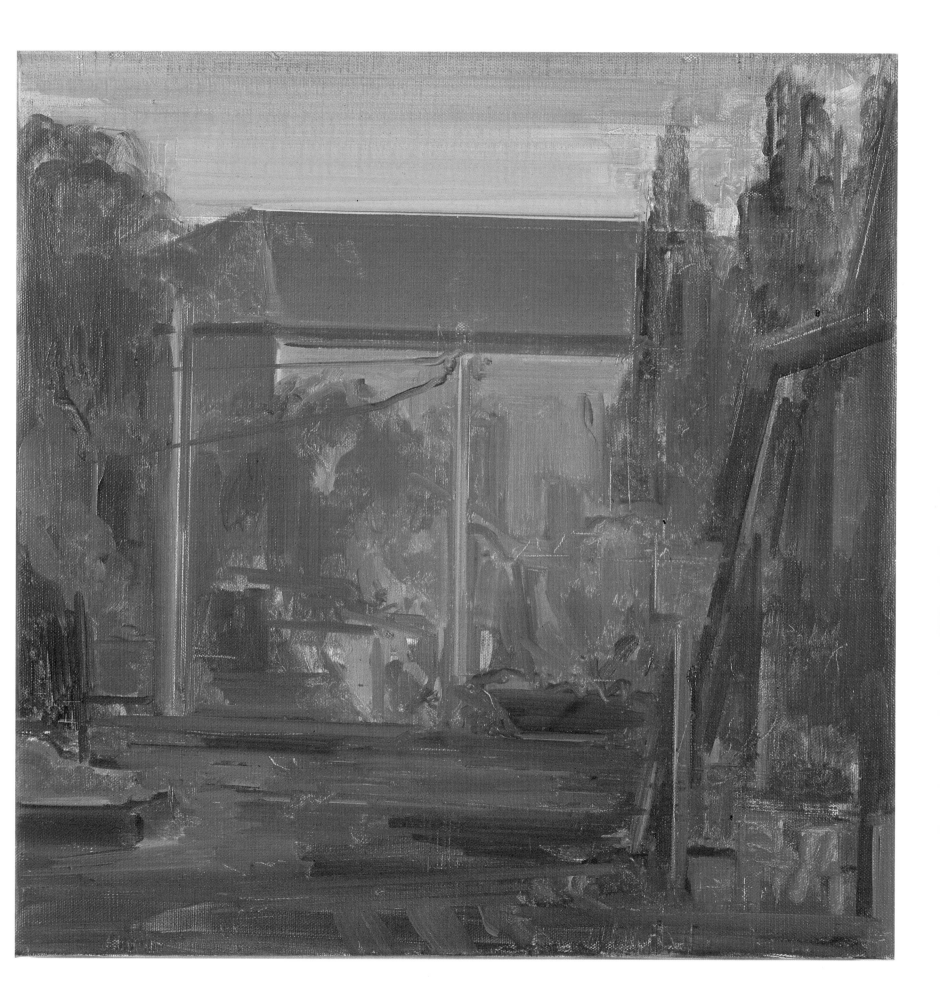

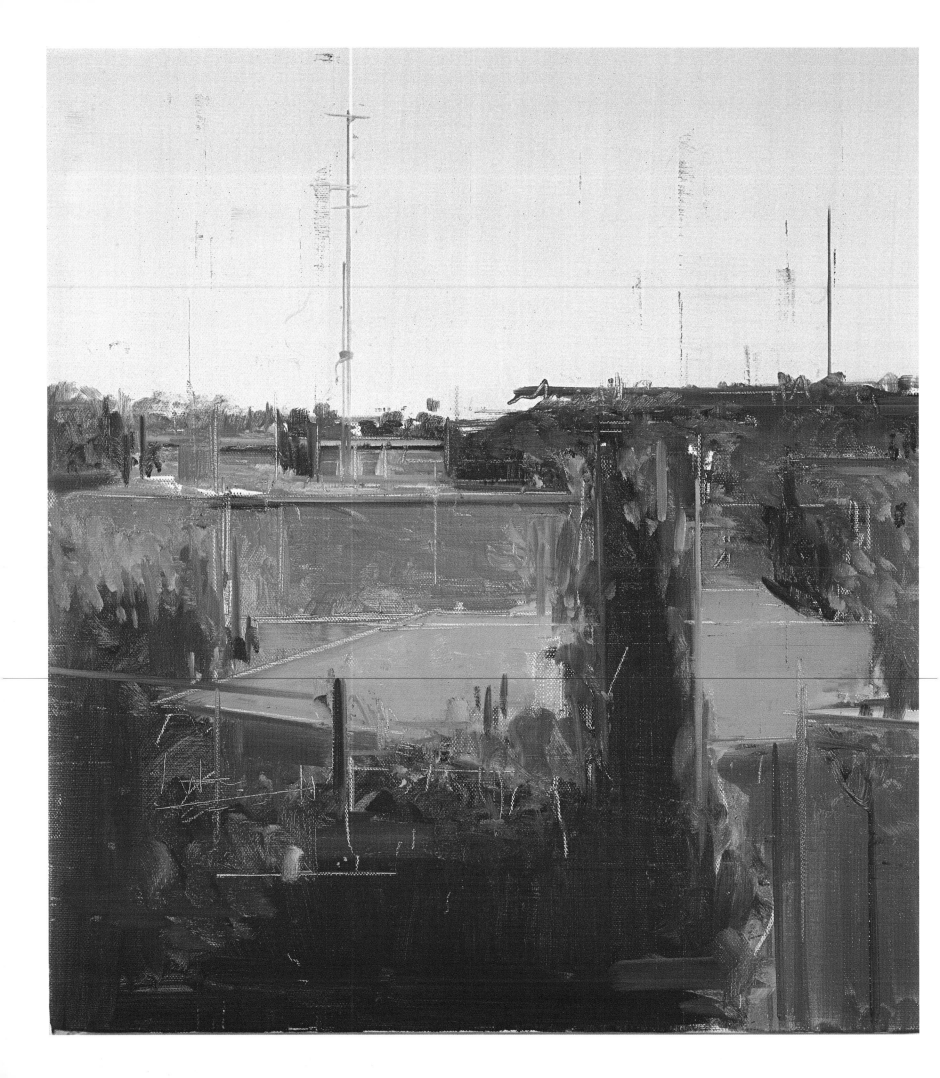

CHAPTER THIRTEEN

Every good café is a living entity with a living dialogue that takes place there—one without words on the whole between a man and himself, and between a man and the people who surround him. At Café Peter, Mrs. Ilana Munk welcomed you with motherly seriousness. Her dishes were simple, rustic, and generous. Usually, she was both the cook and the waitress. The regulars became members of the family. She was aware that I slipped into other cafés, and she would remind me that there had been a time when I had sat only at Café Peter.

In the winter of 1956, my friend Zauber passed away. His widow asked me to say something at the graveside. I was taken aback by her request. It turned out that they were very much alone in Israel, and I, who had met Zauber by chance at Café Rehavia, was considered (by his widow at any rate) as someone close to him.

I liked him very much, and in the course of time I learned to appreciate his game of chess. On the whole, his cautiousness served him well, but sometimes my adventurousness would bring about the impossible and I would win. I liked his tall lankiness, his slender body, and the way his hands moved on the board. He gave the game of chess a kind of ritual seriousness. I knew nothing about him. At Café Rehavia, unlike other cafés, people neither talked of feelings nor revealed personal details.

Less than ten people had gathered at his grave. Were it not for the Burial Society, I would have had to bring in people from off the street. I think it was my first public appearance, and it took place in the open air. I had spent quite a few hours thinking about what I should say. Because I didn't know much about the man and what he had done in his life, I read three poems by Else Lasker-Schuller. From sheer embarrassment and stupidity I added that Mr. Zauber had drawn my attention to the works of Kleist, and for that I would be indebted to him for the rest of my life.

Zauber's sudden death, and the part I played in his funeral, bound me to him. It was as if his presence clung to mine. Whenever I write about tall people (and I often write about them), it's as if he's standing in front of me. Zauber, like so many of those living in Rehavia, came from a long line of assimilated Jews. Hitler forced these assimilated Jews to become Jews. Those who had the misfortune to remain there spent their last days in the camps with the Jews of Eastern Europe, whom they had tried to avoid their whole lives. Even those who came to Israel were not happy to be among Jews. The struggle, the ambiguity over their identity, made them turn inward and made them harsh, cut off from what was around them and often their own worst enemies.

Zauber was not a Zionist; even his Jewishness was tenuous. His prolonged silence, if I understood it correctly, said: "I am what I am, I don't have the strength for an exhaustive soul-search of what I've done and where I've gone wrong. I was a loyal German citizen and I served the country I was born in faithfully. The country of my birth didn't like me and I fled from it in time. In the final analysis, I do not belong here, and I find the whole Jewish business extremely wearying. However, I do love literature and music—they're my country and homeland."

CHAPTER FOURTEEN

Zauber passed away, but I continued to sense his presence on Ibn Gabriel and on Elharizi streets, where I had sometimes met him when he was alive. Professor Hugo Bergman, who taught philosophy, would get very worked up about death notices that included the words, "is no more." "'Is no more?' What does that mean?" he would ask. "Until now he was and now is no longer? Just because we no longer see him—is he no more? A man who has lived continues to live, unless we erase him from our consciousness."

Sometimes it seemed to me that his thoughts were more profound, that perhaps he wrote them down at night in his notebooks. His widow, whom I met at Café Rehavia a month after his death, told me straightforwardly, "Manfred didn't write. He loved to read and to listen to music."

"And what was his hobby?" I probed.

"Greek and Latin. He had taken these languages at the university for three years and proved an outstanding student. His father's death forced him to stop studying and made him responsible for the family's factory—cardboard boxes. He loved the classics, and would read a chapter or two every day."

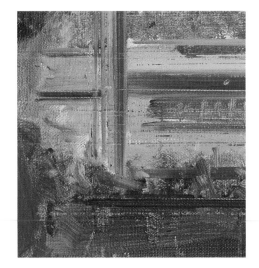

My connection with Zauber had been our weekly chess game. This allowed me to gaze at him from up close, and he is imprinted on my consciousness. Being close does not always connect people. Sometimes the links of silence are deeper. At any rate, Zauber, despite passing away, is a living presence for me. Even now, his long hand, hesitating, continues to hover in front of my eyes. Sometimes it seems to me that, through his silence, he has transferred some important principle to me that helps me and gives me support.

And for a moment it seemed to me that not only I, but she too, wondered at the secret of the man with whom she had lived for thirty years—who was he really, and why had he left the world prematurely? But in Rehavia during this period, feelings and thoughts were well concealed, and everyone remained a secret unto himself.

After his death, and after the brief meeting with his widow, I no longer continued frequenting Café Rehavia. During the 1950s, I started going to Café Pat. Again, I don't recall who first brought me there. Perhaps I discovered it by myself. Café Pat was at the corner of The Street of the Prophets, where it met Kook Street. It was opposite Ethiopia Street, with its Ethiopian Church. I had never counted myself among church enthusiasts. During the war, the churches and monasteries did not throw open their gates to

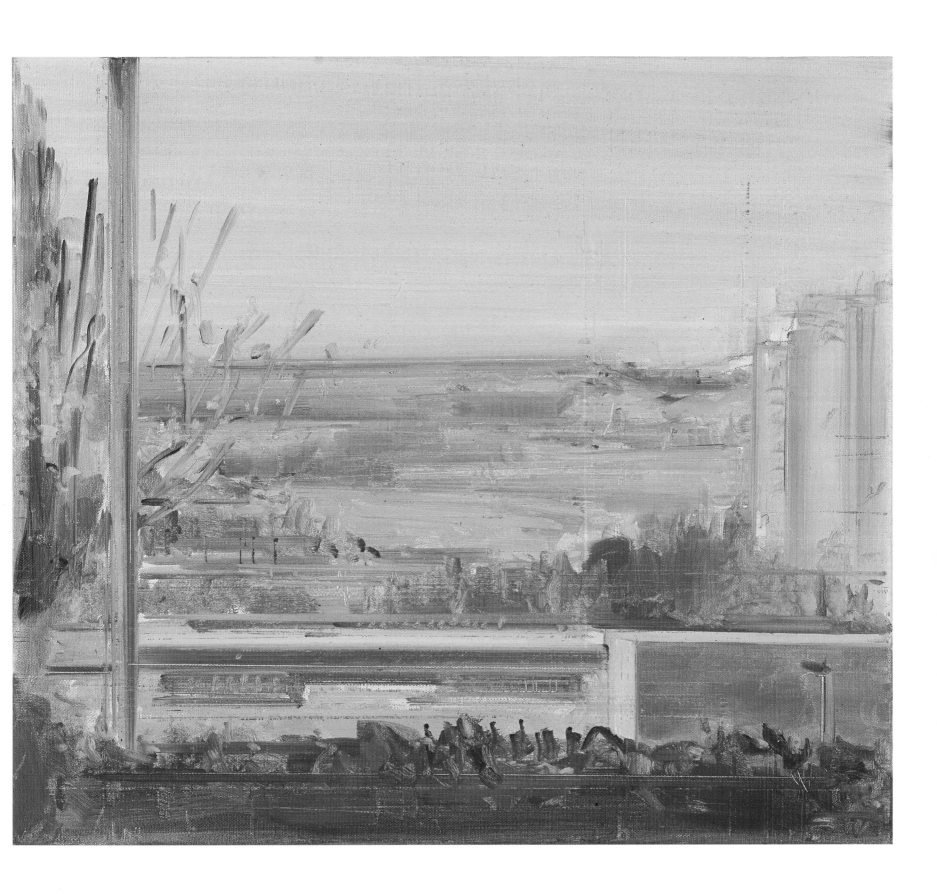

"Imaginary or from experience?"

"That's hard for me to answer."

"Why?"

"Everything's from experience, but not in the order that it took place," and on the spot, I attempted to summarize my approach to writing.

"Where were you in the war?"

I told him.

"I've heard about Transnistria."

He also thought it was hard to write about the Holocaust, since what happened to us was beyond belief. It's hard to speak of the *un*believable, since people might think you're making it up, or even worse, lying. When I told him that I was learning Yiddish, his face rounded in astonishment. "With whose encouragement? Who's behind you?"

"There was no need for encouragement."

"Czernowitz was a city of assimilated Jews, wasn't it?"

"True."

"May God look after you." He spoke to me as people who believed in God would speak a generation ago.

Before he left the café, he came up to me, put a wad of banknotes on my table and said to me, "That's for you." When I refused to accept the money he said, "You can't refuse them. That's my thanks and my gift for your studies. You should know that if someone studies Yiddish in our day, I feel I have to show my appreciation—almost to take my hat off to him."

And that's what he actually did, and wouldn't let me say another word.

me: on more than one occasion I was roughly pushed away. But the Ethiopian Church has always stirred my imagination. There is a kind of innocence to their worship of God. The structure of the church, the icons, the rugs, the colorful windows—all make me think of a temple built by children.

Café Pat combined a bakery and a café. The clientele at Café Pat were traders, agents, moneychangers, and Jews who bridged the religious neighborhood of Meah Shearim with secular Jaffa Street. At Café Pat, transactions took place that required silence and discretion. Envelopes passed from hand to hand, and sometimes dollars could be glimpsed between the hands. The old Jewish way of life continued here with the same expressions and hand gestures. I had seen these Jews before the war, and I had seen them in the ghetto and the concentration camp. They had not changed. The Zionist dream had not transformed them. Again, I never judge other people by moral standards or a Zionist yardstick. Whoever was in the Holocaust learned that there are people who will not harm you, but who will also not offer you a crumb from their rations. People who are considered "decent" can be indifferent, entrenched within their egotism. On more than one occasion, I was taken in and looked after by shady dealers—people who, by all criteria, would be considered outside the law. But during the war it was they, and not the "decent" people, who offered me a crust of bread and shelter. And in the period of chaos and confusion right after the war, the thugs were the ones who protected the children. But besides this, I like dealers and money changers. Behind their gray facade, there can be a solid character. A dealer knows how people tick, and he understands human foibles. If you've come to ask his advise, he won't tell you: "That's illegal," but rather advise you how to avoid getting into trouble. Naiveté is not for them; they are also a reservoir of irony and humor.

"What are you writing?" asked one of the dealers who noticed that I sometimes come into Café Pat and sit there writing for some hours.

"Stories," I told him, not trying to conceal it.

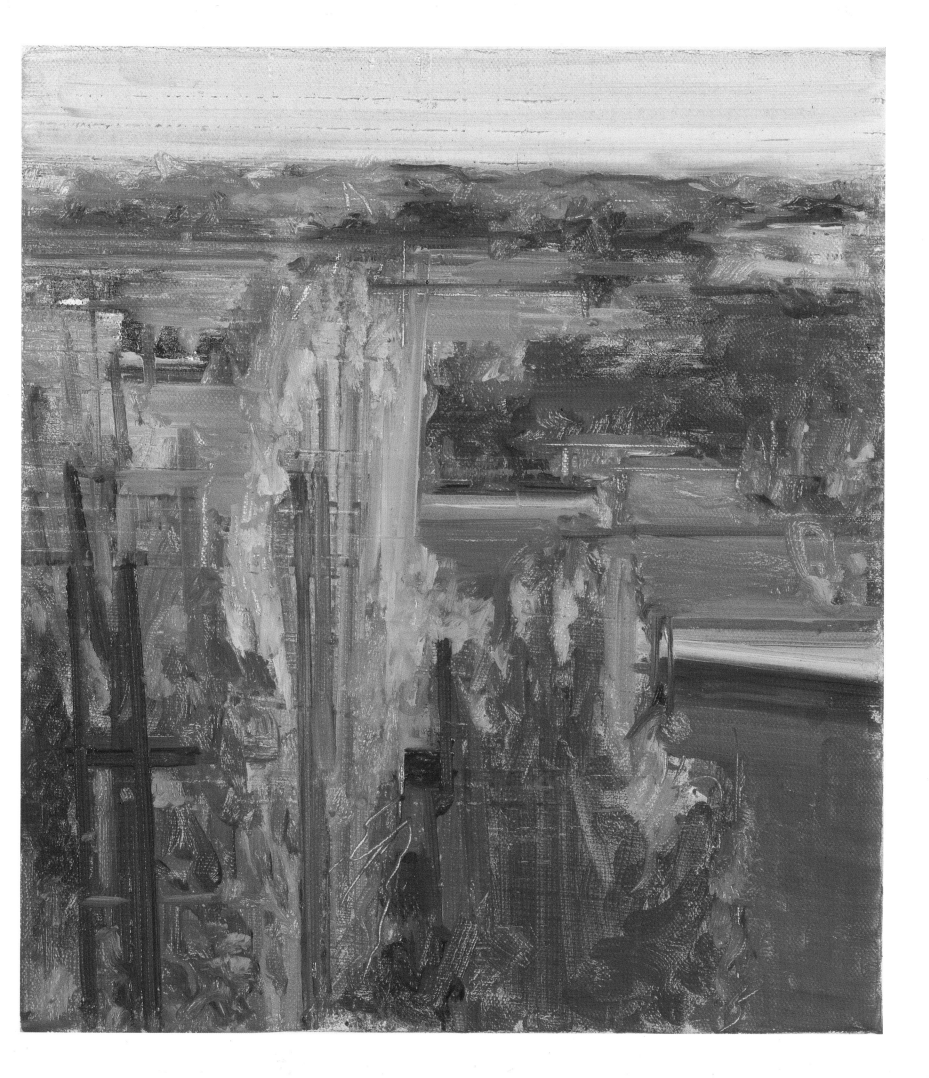

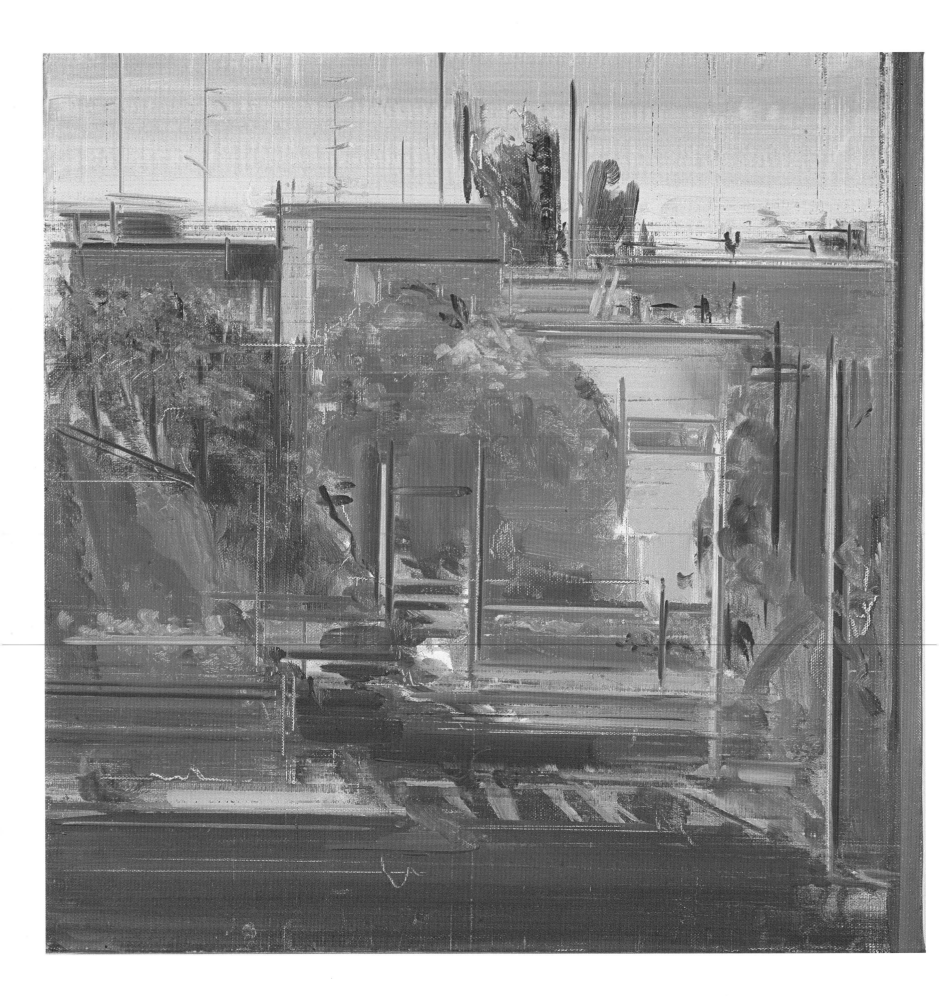

CHAPTER FIFTEEN

I usually went to Café Peter. But once a week I would patronize Café Pat. Most of the traders who frequented it had come after the war; some of them still retained gestures from their religious homes. They spoke Yiddish, with a sentence in Hebrew, or an occasional word in Polish thrown in. In Café Pat the Holocaust was more tangible. Unlike Café Peter, here things were in the open. Painful memories would emerge raw, but for the most part people dealt in the practical: dollars bought and sold, gold coins. The years of the post-war refugee camps continued here and found a good foothold.

After Zauber's death I kept going to Café Hermon from time to time. Once a month I would come to see Shlomo Zemach, who was extremely dignified in his old age. Zemach, whose tongue was like a razor, would be sharply dressed and with the utmost care. He aimed his barbs at Agnon. He liked neither the man nor his writing, and was indignant that Agnon had been made into the oracle of Hebrew literature.

Café Peter was my home; I knew that a wicker chair always awaited me there in the right-hand corner. However, at Café Pat, I had to make it fit my needs. Not every table is advantageous for writing. It's preferable that you can see from your corner, without being too exposed. If you are exposed, you'll be seen, you'll be watched, and eventually you'll be disturbed. Café Pat belonged to another time and place; it brought up the ghosts of war—gaping buildings, crowded railway stations, people who want to say something yet find themselves choked. Sometimes I had the feeling that the traders were about to bend down, pick up their backpacks and be on their way.

At Café Peter, too, the Holocaust would be mentioned but it was swallowed up, wrapped in little courtesies, and what was left unsaid loomed larger than what was said. The Austro-Hungarian Empire lingered on at Café Peter, and the survivors flitted like shadows across it.

At Café Peter nuances were revealed to me, the oddness and contradictions of life: In one corner is a young woman attracted to a man many years older than herself; in another corner there is a couple whose conjugal life must have fallen apart long ago, yet they continue to live together and get on each other's nerves. And right next to this couple, a man whose every movement oozes loneliness; in yet another corner a couple, far from young, who celebrate love with an abandon that makes onlookers envious.

I also saw sights like these in the transit camps on the way to Israel. But that was in the midst of tremendous chaos, and I was a child. Then, at the age of twenty-eight, I found the same sights revealed to me in the garden of a quiet Jerusalem café.

At a time when the newspapers and the radio blared away with hacks talking in pompous phrases, and the political parties were inciting people with their slogans, Café Peter served as a shelter for all those whom life had wounded. It was a wonderful shelter. Those who were fortunate drank from the cup of love, while some just sat and read books, while others jotted things down in a notebook, and a man who was not young sat in the garden, smoking one cigarette after another.

Those were the years that I taught at a night school. The students

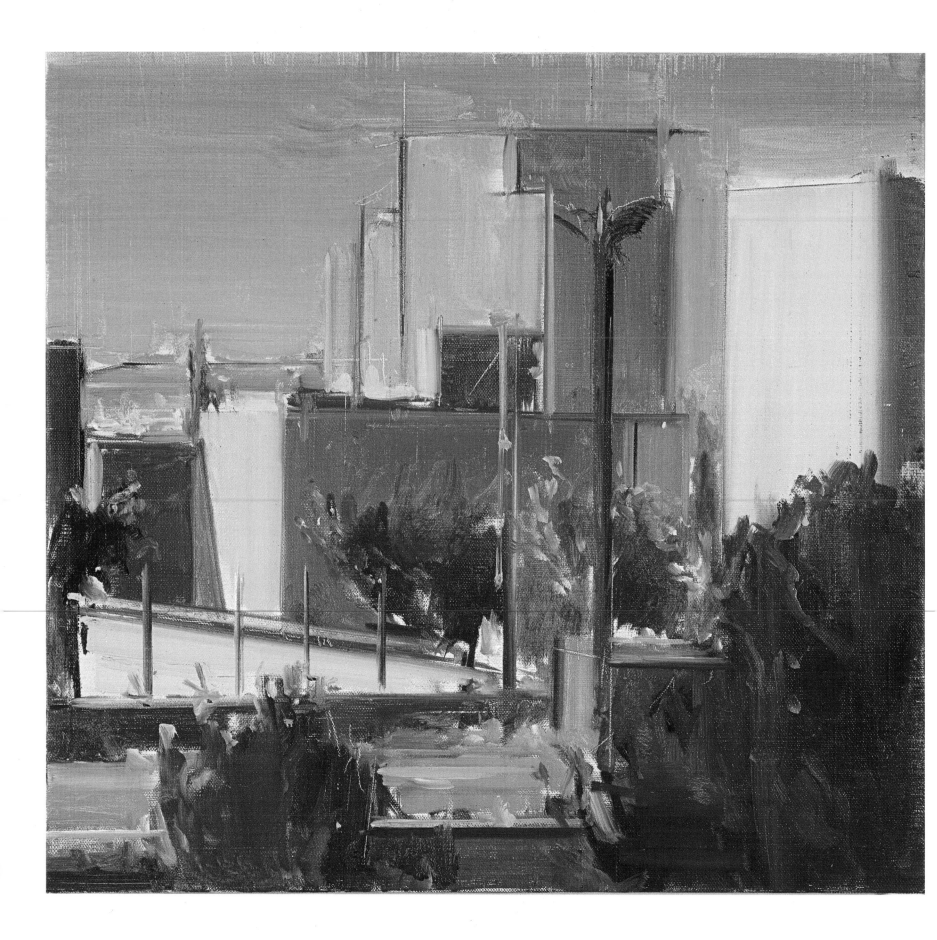

were young, already working hard, and in the evenings they would come straight from the workshops and the garages, tired and utterly worn out. The last thing that they wanted to hear was my interpretation of Bialik's "City of Slaughter". After an hour of utter havoc, some of them would doze off on the benches; those who had stayed awake would sit and listen quite passively.

It was a thankless task. Every evening I would return to my room tired and despairing. But even this experience had its gratifying moments. On several occasions, a young guy would come up to me and ask me to forgive him for having fallen asleep. Once a girl of around fifteen approached me and said, "I would like to be a writer. What do I have to do?"

"What would you like to write about?" I asked.
"About my mother," her answer came quickly.

And immediately I saw that the suffering of her mother was imprinted on all her limbs.

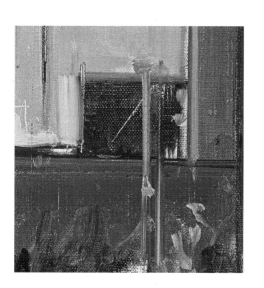

CHAPTER SIXTEEN

I would also set out on walks from Café Pat. I've already mentioned the Ethiopian church on Ethiopia Street. From there I would walk down to Meah Shearim. Here, Jewish history had been frozen within the clothes of the living. Since discovering this area, I would return there every week. It became one of my schools for Jews and Jewishness. Here I learned Yiddish from the mouths of young children and from the old people who sat in the synagogues and learned a page of Talmud with a chanting singsong. The sight of children studying like this—just as they learned throughout the generations in Europe—always moves me. In Meah Shearim, the Holocaust isn't mentioned, but it hovers constantly in the background, the warp of memory that begins in the early hours of the morning and carries on throughout the day, until late at night. Here, and perhaps only here, people speak, pray, and study exactly as they used to in the *shtetls* and cities of Eastern Europe. This act of preservation, even if it is bound up in routine and has some annoying aspects—still commands my respect.

Yiddish was the language of my grandparents, and I always harbored a secret affection for it. This was the secret between me and the world that my parents tried to prevent me from entering. No wonder this isolated tribe, and everything it embodies, has attracted me.

In those years I felt a connection to those on the fringes, to émigrés who had come from my area and whom I met in Café Peter, to those who had come from Germany and shut themselves away in their own ghetto in Rehavia, and those pushed aside in Meah Shearim. Every time I said I was learning Yiddish, people would react with either amazement or silence. Yiddish represented everything that Zionism rejected: the Diaspora, anomalous lives, crowded towns, ghettos, and concentration camps. I, too, had wanted to escape from all that. After I completed my army service, I had wanted to study agriculture and become a farmer in a collective farm. But my education was an obstacle. When I tried to get into the Faculty of Agriculture at the Hebrew University, I was rejected. Fortunately, I met Dov Sadan at the very outset of my time at the university. He taught Yiddish and Yiddish literature. With his soft-spoken manner, he told me: "Come and join us. We may not be many, but we do keep faith with what fate has dealt us."

It was as if this wise man had peered inside me and guessed exactly what I needed. Meah Shearim was like a mine for me. I would crisscross it, traversing its entire length and breadth, entering the courtyards and the little synagogues. For hours on end I would stand outside the classrooms, eavesdropping on those studying and learning by rote. Meah Shearim was full of bookshops. I would stand in them and read. If I had a spare coin to my name, I would buy a book or two. Hasidism enchanted me more and more. At that time I would frequent the Bratzlav synagogues. I loved the openness there, the anarchy and the sheer joy.

Jewish history was right here; in these repudiated margins. I felt connected to these estranged backwaters of Jerusalem, not only because of the way they clung to anachronism, but also because they were vital to my spiritual life. People easily identify with the mainstream. The mainstream gives them a sense of consensus and security. It is understandable that people fear the margins.

My connection with the Jews of Meah Shearim had its ups and downs, but I never cut myself off from them. To this day, I still go there once or twice a week. I love watching the rhythm of life there; I like to see how much modernity has infiltrated and what has been rejected. There's no lack of contradictions. Sometimes I go into a synagogue and join people studying. Elderly people who respond with intellectual sharpness command my respect. In Meah Shearim there's a difference between everyday talk, and the way people study and the way people pray. These three forms of expression can't be taken for granted. Here I have to confess to a weakness of mine: everything Jewish is dear to me. I learned Yiddish not only in the Hebrew University and in Meah Shearim, but also picked it up in the Yiddish-speaking clubs of the *Bund*. There, too, I discovered love and stubborn loyalty to a different Jewish belief—secular Yiddish—one that had been pushed into the sidelines.

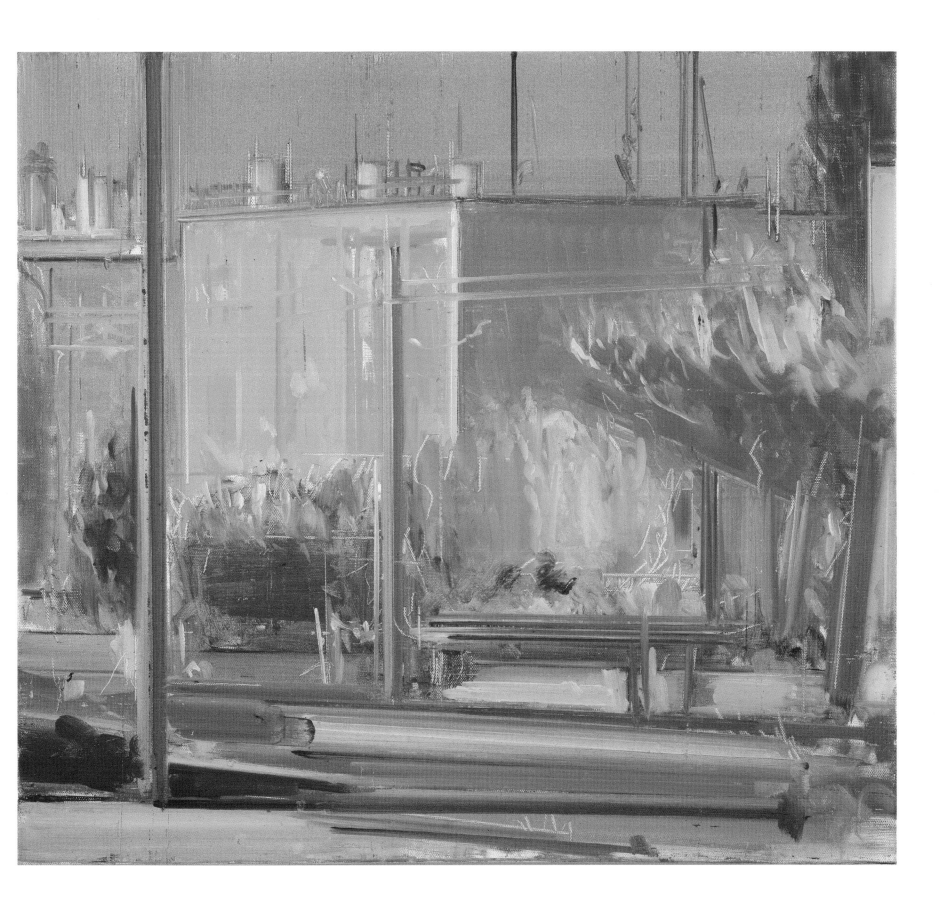

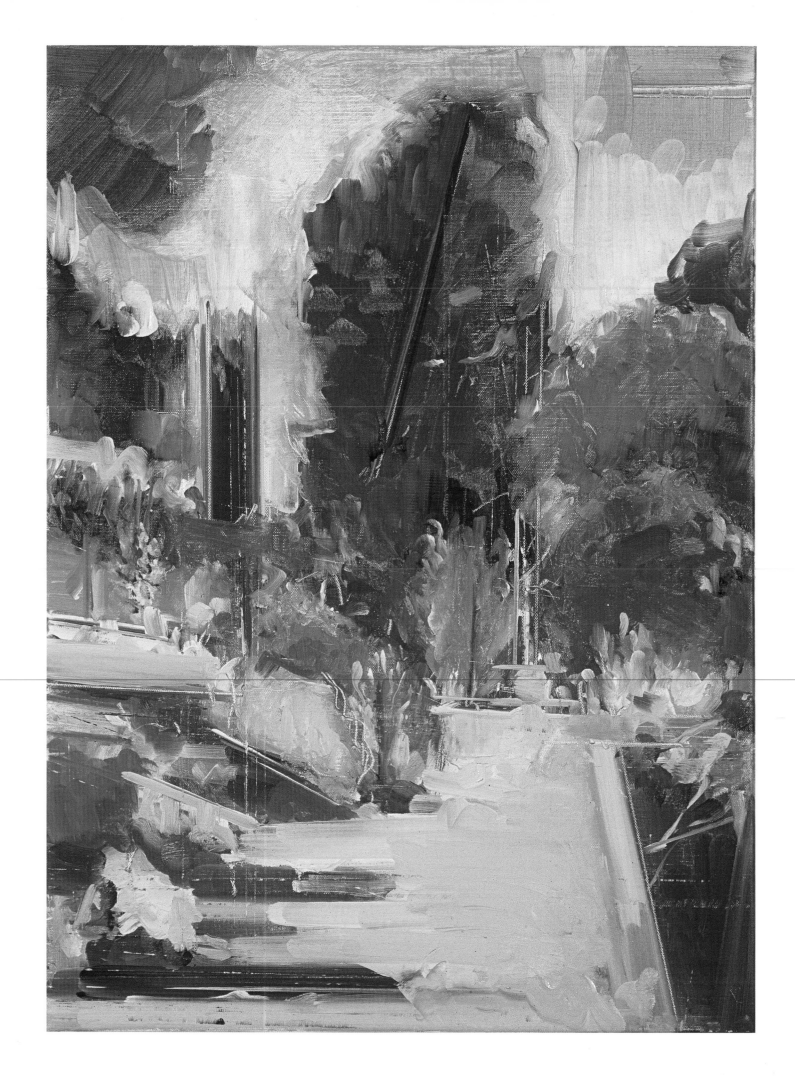

CHAPTER SEVENTEEN

My fellow-townsman, S. is older than me by nine years. A good-looking man, with nice manners, he's very knowledgeable in the history of the region where both of us were born. He was able to finish high school there. I showed him my novella, *Like the Apple of the Eye*, while it was still a manuscript. He read it and prepared a long list of inaccuracies.

"Even though you're not a historian," he said, "it's important to be accurate. Accuracy adds to credibility."
"My stories and novellas come from my private world. I don't write about what was."
"No? So what are they about?"
"What really lives in me from that place, and what remains from those years."
"And yet still you write of the past, don't you?"

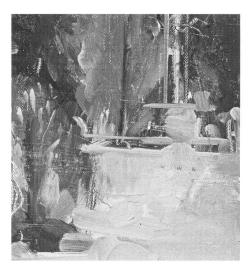

"My time sequence is the present continuous. I write of the city of my birth, yet at the same time I write about Jerusalem. After all, I left my city when I was barely nine years old. I only got to know the people who surrounded me then, when I met people just like them in Jerusalem—in the German Colony, in Katamon, in Rehavia and in Meah Shearim."

"Why not be accurate?"
"I'm no historian. A novella is an accumulation of experience, a chunk of life. It sets out an idea, but it's not a chronicle. My form of accuracy is different from that of the person who writes history. I'm interested in other details. I'm trying to make the past—present; perhaps the future too."

"But all the same, there is a sense of time and place in your books. It's not as if they are without a sense of time, like the stories of Kafka."

"True, but the time and the place are very much my own. Picture a Jewish child, let's say he's seven, sitting on the floor in Czernowitz in 1939. The house is spacious and quiet and he's playing with wooden cubes and with balls. Suddenly he bursts out crying. His mother rushes over to him, hugs and kisses him and asks him to explain why he's crying. The more she tries to calm him down, the stronger he cries. After a long time, the child says, 'I'm afraid.'
"'What are you afraid of? Who are you afraid of? We're the only ones at home.'
"'Of the lions.' The words come out.

"'The lions are in the forest, there aren't any lions in the city,' the mother says, sure that she has come up with a response that will calm him. But it's no use, the child just goes on crying.

"The mother is helpless. Eventually she says, 'You're a big boy and you know that there aren't any lions in the city. Lions either live in the forest or are shut away in cages in the zoo.'

"It's true that both time and place exist in my stories and in my novellas, but they are extremely private, almost secret. The child of seven has picked up the disquiet in his home and he's in great anxiety about what is to come. For him, this great dread takes the form of lions. Less than a year will pass and human beasts *will* overrun his home, devouring most of those living in it. Yet it isn't a prophecy, but an existential fear.

CHAPTER EIGHTEEN

"My accuracy focuses on the micro and not the macro. To me, it's important to describe the parquet floor, the muslin curtains, the spacious living room, the quiet and the pleasant softness of a petit-bourgeois house. The child suddenly feels that very soon he'll lose everything good and pleasant. In my own home, in 1939, there was talk of financial problems, political problems, about emigration and fleeing the trap, but all these complex matters were too lofty for me to understand. For me, fear took the form of lions. That was within the scope of my imagination.

"With an artist, what's very private paradoxically becomes universal. A child's fear, to go back to the example that I've given, is fear that's linked to 1939, but at the same time it's the eternal fear in the face of the unknown, which we all carry within us."

Since the publication of my first story, I've been treated as if I were the chronicler of the Holocaust. I'm not someone writing a chronicle, nor am I a historian. I try to be a novelist. What is important for the historian does not concern me. The historian makes a distinction between one place and another, between past and present. I do not distinguish between them. In this respect, and not only in this respect, the artist continues to be a child. For him, what was "then" and what is "now" are intertwined. There was a right-wing critic who claimed that I refuse to relinquish the trauma of childhood and insist on bringing it here. Another critic, this time a left-winger, claimed that my writing on the Holocaust inflames nationalistic sentiments. Such allegations will only flourish in a country constantly in the throes of ideological obsessions.

There were years when I suffered from this. But as I grow older, it becomes increasingly clear to me: You simply have to be yourself. Just that.

Summer. 1963. After a month of army reserve duty, I returned with absolutely no idea what I was going to do. It was as if the ground had been swept away from beneath me. It had been a month of continuous guard duty, day and night. Stiflingly hot in the day, and at night, the cold of the desert. Once a month a guarded convoy would make its way to Mount Scopus and after that we were cut off from the rest of the world for an entire month. A small island in a sea of enmity. While I was on guard duty at Mount Scopus, I wasn't afraid, but since my return I've been dreaming that a horde of Arabs are at the outpost, overrunning it, and that our guns have jammed.

I sit at Café Peter, but what I've seen in the Judean desert passes before my eyes. During the first days at the outpost, I was enchanted by the desert colors. I was certain that these spiritual hills would enrich me and that I would return completely changed. I was wrong. I share this isolated outpost with three other soldiers, taking over from one another on shifts of guard duty, eating sardines and stale bread. After a few days, not only were the landscapes far from enchanting, but I would shut my eyes so as not to see them.

Over the years I had grown accustomed to tough periods of training, but to be shut up for an entire month with three soldiers who spend most of their time cursing life and cursing army reserve duty, is far harder than any exhausting training under the relentless sun.

The poet Yehoshua Tan-Pai would come to Café Peter, and I was always glad to see him. Tan-Pai was some fifteen years older than me. A man who had suffered much, he never talked about his sor-

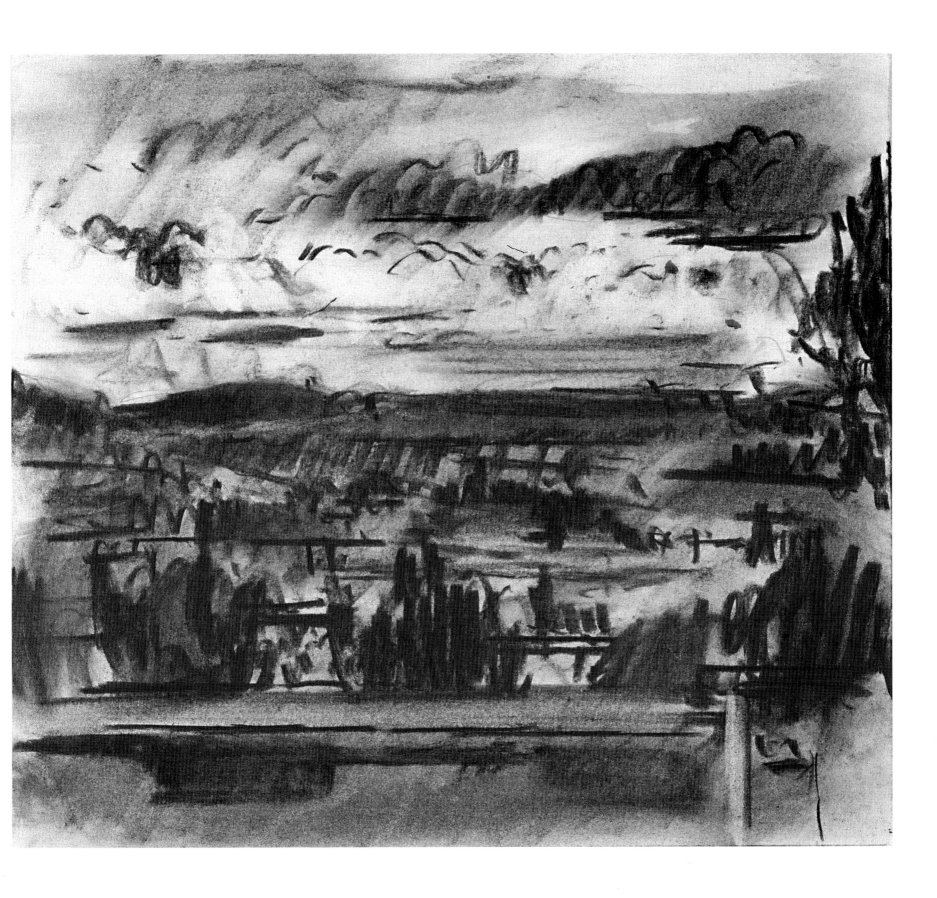

row. If he spoke, he spoke about his weaknesses. He always took an interest in what I was reading and what I was writing. He had the nobility of a man who has conquered his own sorrow. Tall, pleasant looking, his slight limp only added grace to his stature; he was generous and aristocratic in the full sense of the word.

When Tan-Pai started writing, he had been influenced by Natan Alterman, but in the course of time, he formulated his own distinct style. Sorrow purified and crystallized his poems. I told him about my experiences at Mount Scopus, and how detached I felt toward my reading and my notebooks. He listened and advised me to leave everything and to go out and just walk around. "A walk is a good preparation for every new connection."

"A day in Rehavia?" I asked.
"No."
"Where?"
"Meah Shearim. Sit in one of the small synagogues and take in a lesson on *Gemarah*. After a day in Meah Shearim you'll find your way back."

Strange, that was also my feeling. Like me, he also loved the Jews of previous generations.

We spoke about Jerusalem neighborhoods and about the Judean desert. I admitted: "I am more drawn to modern Jerusalem than to the historical city. I feel a sense of belonging to modern Jerusalem. Even though each neighborhood speaks to me in a different language, they nevertheless are languages I recognize. Historical Jerusalem speaks in a language of prophecies and visions. There's no doubt that the Temple and prophecy are the pinnacle of faith, but only metaphysical poetry can attain such heights. Prose needs

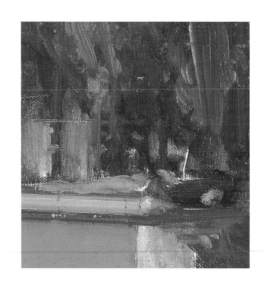

solid ground; it needs objects and a space whose dimensions you can relate to. The peaks of prophecy and revelation are just not possible in prose. Biblical prose, in contrast to prophecy, is factual; it recognizes the weaknesses of man and does not demand divine attributes of flesh and blood. One can listen to the prophets, but it's impossible to draw near to them."

Tan-Pai did not agree with me. He promised me that one day the poetry of the prophets would be as close to my heart as the prose of the Bible, since they were one, and that moreover, modern Jerusalem without the historical Jerusalem was an ugly city, lacking in culture and taste. What graced her wretchedness was that the historical city lay beneath her.

Tan-Pai would usually frequent Café Atara but when we met, he would usually come to Café Peter or Café Pat. He loved the freshly baked pastries at Café Pat and the merchants who crowded around the small tables. He also had a warm affinity to these people on the fringes of society. We would often sit together and gaze at them. The Jews and commerce—the blessing and the curse, wrapped together.

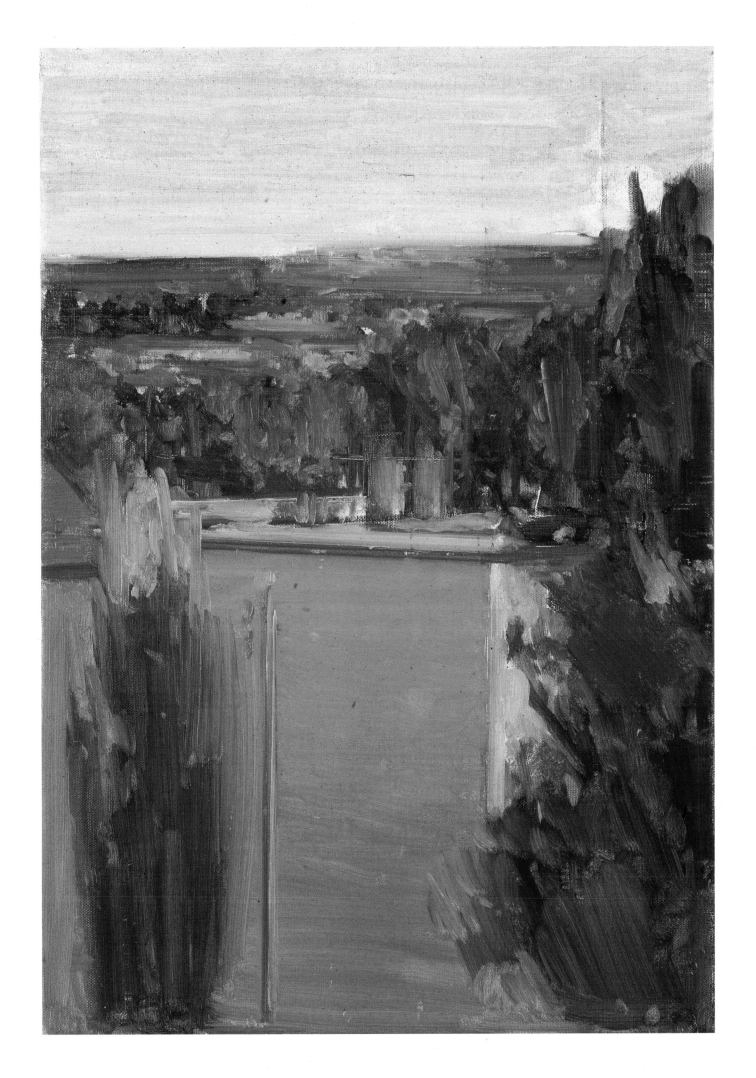

CHAPTER NINETEEN

Most of the day I'm on my own, busy writing. Among other things, writing demands great attentiveness that goes on for hours. There are days when I can't produce so much as a paragraph, and what I put down is bland or amorphous. Days like that mean the agony of treading water and self-recrimination. Then it's preferable to be doing some physical work, to go out on a long stint army reserve duty—anything to get away from my scribbling. On several occasions a long sleep has saved me from this torture.

But there are days when you are tethered to the table—writing. Thoughts and words come together; the right sentences rise up as if by themselves. One sentence pulls another sentence after it, and eventually you have a picture or an idea. On such days you are full of anxious happiness and at the end of the day you feel like saying a blessing.

Once I met Haim Hazaz in the street and he asked how I was. I told him: "Thank God."
"Why do you say 'thank God?'" he said, harshly. "Are you religious?"
I didn't know what to say and I made a gesture of embarrassment.
"An author has to be very careful about what he says."
I agreed with him.

His reproach gnawed at me. Since I've been writing, I have tried to make the words fit the intention. That time I failed.

According to accepted norms, I would not be considered a religious Jew. I neither go to synagogue nor do I keep the commandments according to the strict letter of the law, but Jewish creativity is indispensible to me: the Bible, the *Mishnah*, the *Gemarah*, the literature of the medieval period, the mystics and hasidic literature are all my books. I study them daily for an hour or two, sometimes more. They accompany my waking thoughts.

Whenever I have to go abroad for a short time, I put two books in my bag. One, a work of Kafka, and the other, chapters of the mystics or a hasidic text. I can't be without a Jewish book. I love the Russian classics and some works of modern literature, but I have this intimate connection to Jewish books. They are as necessary to me as air to breathe.

Once Yeshayahu Tishby, who would sometimes come into Café Hermon, saw me sitting and studying *Likutei Moharan*, a hasidic classic. He came up to me and said, musingly "That's a difficult book; what do you get from it?"
"An attitude to the world."
"Are you a religious man?"
"Yes," I said, and I was happy that I said it.

I found his direct question annoying. It was as if he were looking for a defect or something that was wrong in me. I live Jewish life in my own way. I love observant Jews and have cause to love them. During the war, all Jews were tortured, but observant Jews were singled out for greater torture and ridicule. Their beards and sidelocks were sometimes plucked off from their faces, they could

CHAPTER TWENTY

be forced to crawl naked on all fours while pork was forced into their mouths. You cannot forget such sights.

My grandfather was an observant Jew. When I think of him or write about him, I find myself embracing his gestures. And there are moments when I know that real prayer is only possible when you are wrapped in a prayer shawl. I have no pretensions of being observant, but it's impossible to deny my connection to prayer, to the *mitzvot*, customs— not to speak of the books—only because I don't keep them in their entirety.

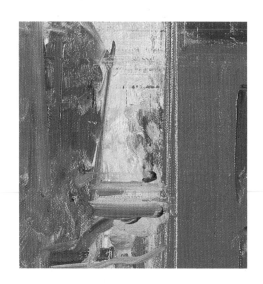

From the mid-1960s, I began to go to Café Atara on Ben Yehuda Street. Marriage didn't change my habits. On the days that I wasn't working, or rather, during the hours that I wasn't working, I would sit in a café. Occasionally I would try to sit in a library. There, the thunderous silence muted my thoughts. I would sit there, or gaze at those leafing through books looking for an article or a quotation, and finally I would leave in confusion and distress.

Café Atara was not like Café Peter. Most of the day it was milling with people, but its upper floor was quiet and there was a corner by the window where my imagination conjured up the sights I needed. After a few hours of writing, I would take a stroll, walking up to Agrippas Street, meandering about for an hour or two. Then I would return home. The stroll was a continuation of the writing. On every walk I would recall some word that had eluded me, some phrase, or I would remove an obstacle that was obstructing the plot.

It was rather late in life that I learned the simple rule that a story is not a description. Even the most successful description cannot stand on its own; it's static and holds up the flow. A story has to have a beginning, a middle and an end; it must flow at all costs. I learned this rule in fact not from the Russian classics but from the stories of Kafka. Because he dealt with mystery, Kafka was extremely careful about reality. His short stories are sometimes borne on the back of a raging river.

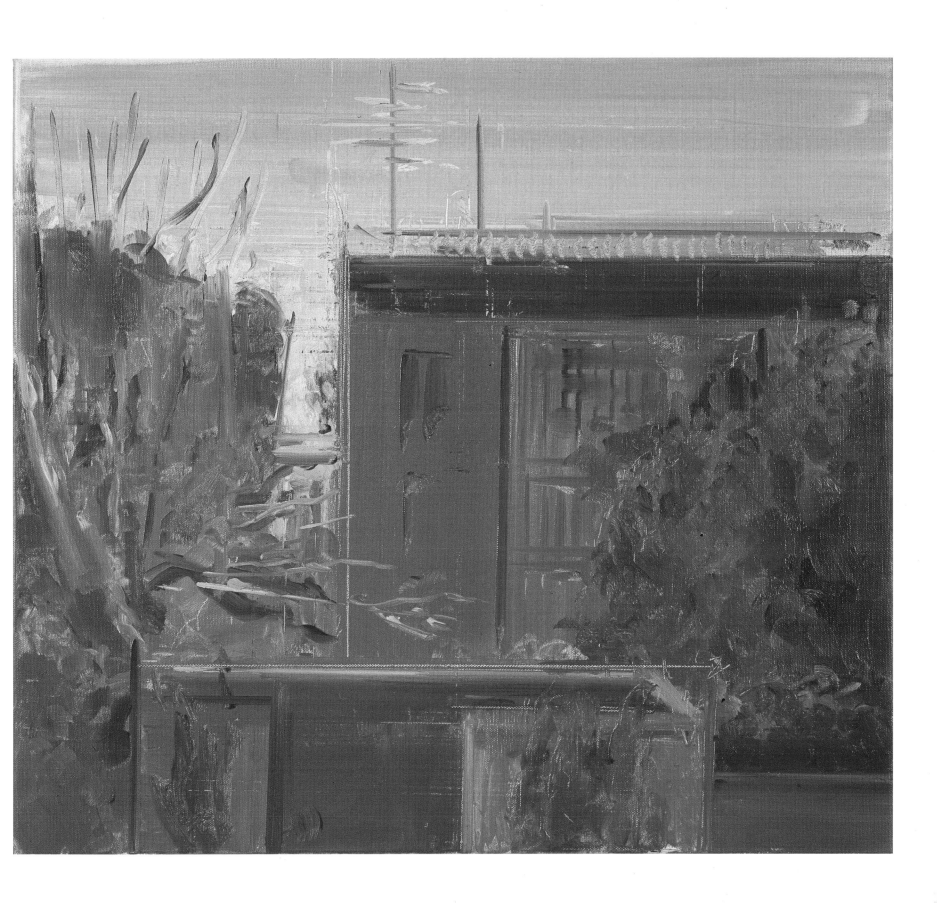

At Café Atara, I would meet Shai Agnon, Haim Hazaz, Arieh Lipshitz, Shalom Kramer, Haim Toren and Yehoshua Tan-Pai—all of them now in the Land of Truth. I was the youngster in this circle, which meant I had the privilege of looking on, following what was said and keeping silent. To this very day, I don't feel that comfortable amid a group of people. There are some artists who come to life within a circle of people, even without a glass of cognac. I prefer to sit and talk to another person quietly, and even then I prefer to listen rather than be listened to. Agnon, as is well known, was neither modest nor silent. His language, even when only talking, dripped irony. And sometimes he would really torture an author or one of his critics. I did not admire his verbal irony or the irony

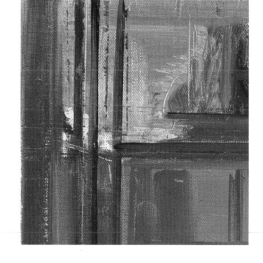

in his writing. I thought then, and still think today, that Agnon's writing is good not so much because of its derision, and not on account of its irony, and not because of its excessive symbolism, but for when that he speaks out directly, identifying with his characters. With Agnon there is a fundamental seriousness—his religiousness, for example. Due to certain critics, he has acquired the name of almost a heretic, at least of someone with an ambivalent relationship to religious belief. This is simply not true. Agnon does deride the dealers, the unscrupulous rabbis and the run-of-the-mill hypocrites and pretenders—but he does not ridicule Jewish belief as such. I do not mean to say that Agnon was an innocent believer, but it's impossible to deny the very real connection that the person who wrote *The Days of Awe* had with a belief in the God of Israel, or to attribute a perpetual ambivalence to him.

At the same time, I was beginning to feel ever more strongly that the short story was choking me. A short story demands brevity and concision; if you don't take this seriously, you'll be mainly crossing things out. I like to cross out, but too much deletion is dispiriting. In the mid-sixties, I wrote, *Like the Apple of the Eye*. It was done

in several drafts, and I had the feeling that I had broken through some barrier. Later Ephraim Broide published it in his magazine *Molad*, and Gershom Scholem warmly congratulated me on it. I was glad that Scholem, who had reservations about new Hebrew writing, had found my novel to his liking. Although I was happy, deep inside I knew that I still had a long way to go. Up to the time of writing *Like the Apple of the Eye* I had mainly dealt with refugees after the war and particularly with refugees in Israel. The alienation and the wanderings were part of me, and I wanted to give them expression in every possible way. From so many wanderers and refugees, I forgot that I once had a home, parents, and warm surroundings, from which I had been torn away. With the story *Like the Apple of the Eye,* I returned to my home as it was before the devastation.

I had planned to write a Jewish family idyll in the Carpathians, recalling the homes of my grandparents and of my parents. But I quickly learned that literature is not merely reenactment. The creative imagination unconsciously mixes the present and the future. Eventually, what emerged from what I wrote was not an idyll, but a nightmare. Ruthenian peasants and poor relations from the other side of the city all swoop down onto a pleasant, well-tended estate. The way of life that had been slowly and faithfully maintained throughout the centuries is torn to shreds. Almost without my consent the horrors of the war seeped into the novella, and took over. In this process, a different truth arose: disintegration from within. In other words, the holocaust before the Holocaust.

The criticism that's so often leveled against me—why don't you write about the here and now?—has not ceased since the publication of *Smoke,* my first book. This criticism, which I must have internalized, has sometimes made me swerve off course. For

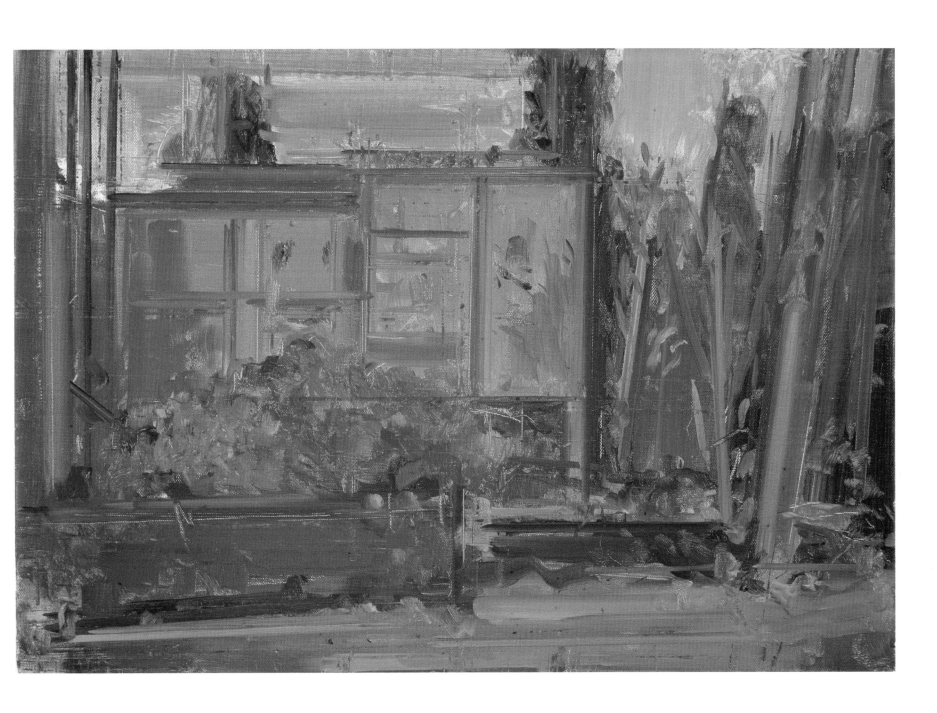

CHAPTER TWENTY-ONE

I met a friend whom I had studied with at university. Like me, he had also dreamed of becoming a writer. There was a time when we would sit for hours at Café Peter. We had often studied for examinations together. We hadn't seen one another for years.

After completing his university studies (my friend S. had graduated with honors, unlike myself), he began managing the family business. He's wealthy, and his elegant appearance—albeit studiously disheveled—bears this out. He lost no time in telling me that he reads my books.

"And what do you think of them?" I asked, unable to contain my curiosity.

"Sad."

"Meaning good or bad?"

"You write for very few people."

"That's bad?" I asked.

"It's not a question of good or bad. My question is this: Why not aim for more popularity?"

He rattled off the names of several Hebrew authors who had become famous in recent years.

"I do what I can," I said, defensively.

"Why aren't you more politically involved?" With this sentence, his criticism was finally out in the open.

example, I was temporarily tempted into writing a novella, *The Skin and the Gown,* with Jerusalem as a backdrop. Here, too, the scenario was the same as when I was writing *Like the Apple of the Eye.* What emerged from my pen was not Jerusalem, but a city flooded by refugees, trapped within a protracted nightmare.

Grusman is sure that his wife had been killed in the war, and then, some twenty years after she's been missing, she comes back, and there she is, standing in the threshold of his room, not the small, slender woman that he remembers, but an ample, sturdy woman. The years in Russia—in Siberia—have molded her into someone heavy-set, solid.

Even this book did not turn out as I'd envisioned. Whenever I tried to ignore my instincts and be what others were asking me to be, the past would immediately rise up and take over what I was doing.

A man cannot escape from himself; he cannot escape his childhood, his parents, and how fate has molded his life. Mostly, I knew this truth and I usually held to it, but there were times when I tried to get away from it, to don a garment that wasn't mine. And then I was punished, compelled to retrace my steps.

I explained at some length why I wasn't, and then I immediately regretted it. My friend S. found it hard to accept my explanation. He kept claiming that a writer cannot allow himself the luxury of standing on the sidelines when crucial events were taking place in Israel, and writers should be part of them. Not only that, he argued,

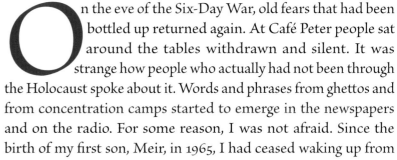

CHAPTER TWENTY-TWO

modern life demands that one speak out loud and clear and not in a mealy-mouthed fashion. Half tones cannot be registered, he said, they're barely heard. It was evident that he had carefully thought out and even rehearsed these words. For a moment I convinced myself that he really was looking out for was my own good. He was trying to advise me in the field that he himself was an expert at: marketing, distribution, and public relations.

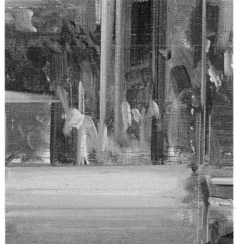

"You're right," I said, "but there's not much hope. It seems like this is just me."
"I understand. And, after all, you do earn a living from your writing," he said, letting out the genie from the bottle.
"No."
"That's a pity."

❦

It pained me that a childhood friend, instead of being happy on my behalf, was looking for my weak points and trying to hurt me. I got up to leave.

"How many hours a day do you write?" he asked me in a different tone.
"Six or seven hours." I didn't hide the truth from him.
"Every day?" he asked.
"Every day."
"Even on days when you work?"
"Yes."
"Excellent—bravo! I work from morning till night and I hardly get to read a book."

And for a moment it seemed to me that in the depths of his heart he envied me, not for my minor successes, but for my ability to persevere and to stand by something that I had started in my youth.

On the eve of the Six-Day War, old fears that had been bottled up returned again. At Café Peter people sat around the tables withdrawn and silent. It was strange how people who actually had not been through the Holocaust spoke about it. Words and phrases from ghettos and from concentration camps started to emerge in the newspapers and on the radio. For some reason, I was not afraid. Since the birth of my first son, Meir, in 1965, I had ceased waking up from nightmares. By now my dreams may not have been quiet, but they were not nightmares. Sometimes my wife would come to visit me at Café Peter, bringing our little son in his stroller. We would sit for a while, and then take a leisurely walk around the German Colony. There were many survivors in the German Colony and Old Katamon, but there wasn't a sense of panic.

Every morning, Tina and her friends would turn up at the usual time. From their faces, I would try to understand what was going on inside them. Inexplicably, they actually appeared calmer than other people in the café. Tina explained to one of her acquaintances: "We aren't afraid any more. We've already used up all our fear, and there's none left for us anymore." Everyone laughed.

Big Arthur emerged from the shell of his silence to comment: "There's no reason that people my age shouldn't be called up to the war. I'm fifty-seven and I can still contribute to the war effort."

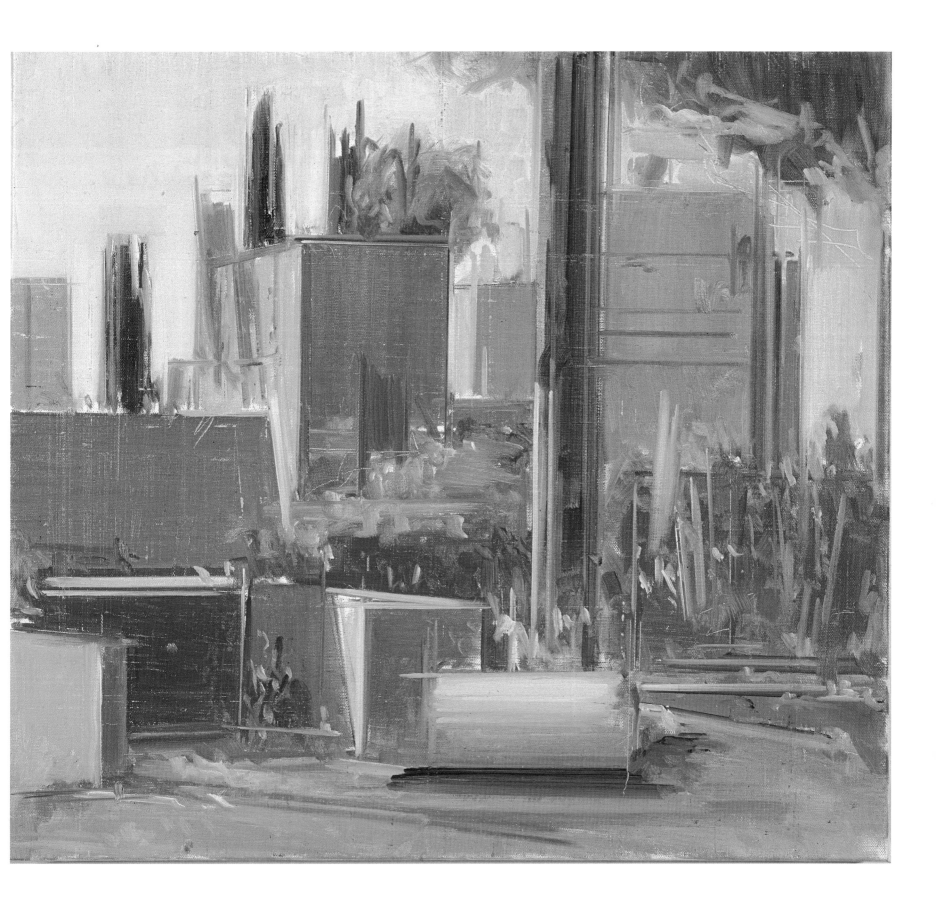

He cannot stand the thought of people younger than himself fighting while he sits at home. In 1946, on his arrival in Israel, he wanted to join the police but was turned down due to his age. For years he worked as a night watchman on building sites. Now he's a pensioner, and thinks back fondly to the days when he was a guard. Once he caught two thieves and that put an end to any thefts on his sites.

The sense of danger intensifies from day to day. People hoard food; everyone is more irritable than usual and prone to sudden outbursts. The prophets of doom have been declaring that our coming to Israel has been useless: it's our fate to be wiped out.

I was called up a few days before the war broke out. It was a swift war. With such a resounding victory, the human losses were swallowed up amid the vast jubilation. Just as the danger and threat had brought to the surface words from the Holocaust, victory brought with it terms from Jewish mysticism. On the radio and in the press people talked of miracles, of Redemption and the coming of the Messiah. These terms were beyond me. I love the mysticism of daily life, the colors and the shadows that surround me, particular spots in Jerusalem toward evening, the light that glints out from the ancient walls and the rocks, the plants that rise out of the parched earth. And even more than them, I love the people who embrace children and the people who pray. This mysticism is close to my heart, but for me cosmic or historical mysticism remains a complete abstraction. My friend Leib Rochman, who always lived on a lofty plane, used to say that I was blind to miracles. I didn't take it as a reproach. When I was a child, my grandfather told me that God dwells everywhere.

"In the trees as well?" I asked.
"In the trees too," he replied.
"In animals too?"
"In animals too."

"In man as well?"
"Man," replied Grandfather, "is the partner of God."
"Man is God?" I was shocked.
"No. But he has a little of God in him."

This conversation has been etched in my memory. Grandfather was a believer—he believed with his whole heart and all his soul. That belief of his was expressed in his every gesture: the way he gripped an object, opened or closed a book, picked up a child and placed him on his knees. Sometimes I feel that I have inherited his religious feelings from him. I never learned much from abstract ideas; the figures from my childhood and the experiences in the Holocaust are what stand before my eyes and have molded my thoughts.

The Six-Day War brought with it much understandable joy, but I found it hard to be happy. Though I'm hardly a gloomy person, there isn't any joy in me; suspicion always flickers there instead. Anyone who went through the Holocaust could not retain his faith in the world.

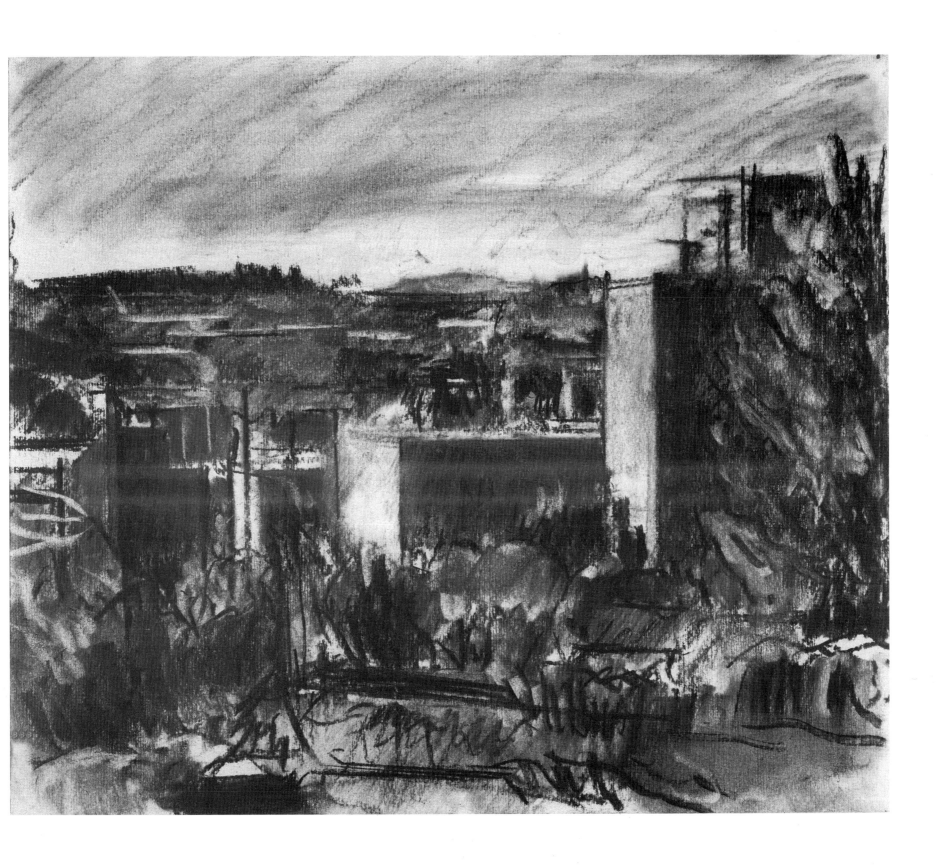

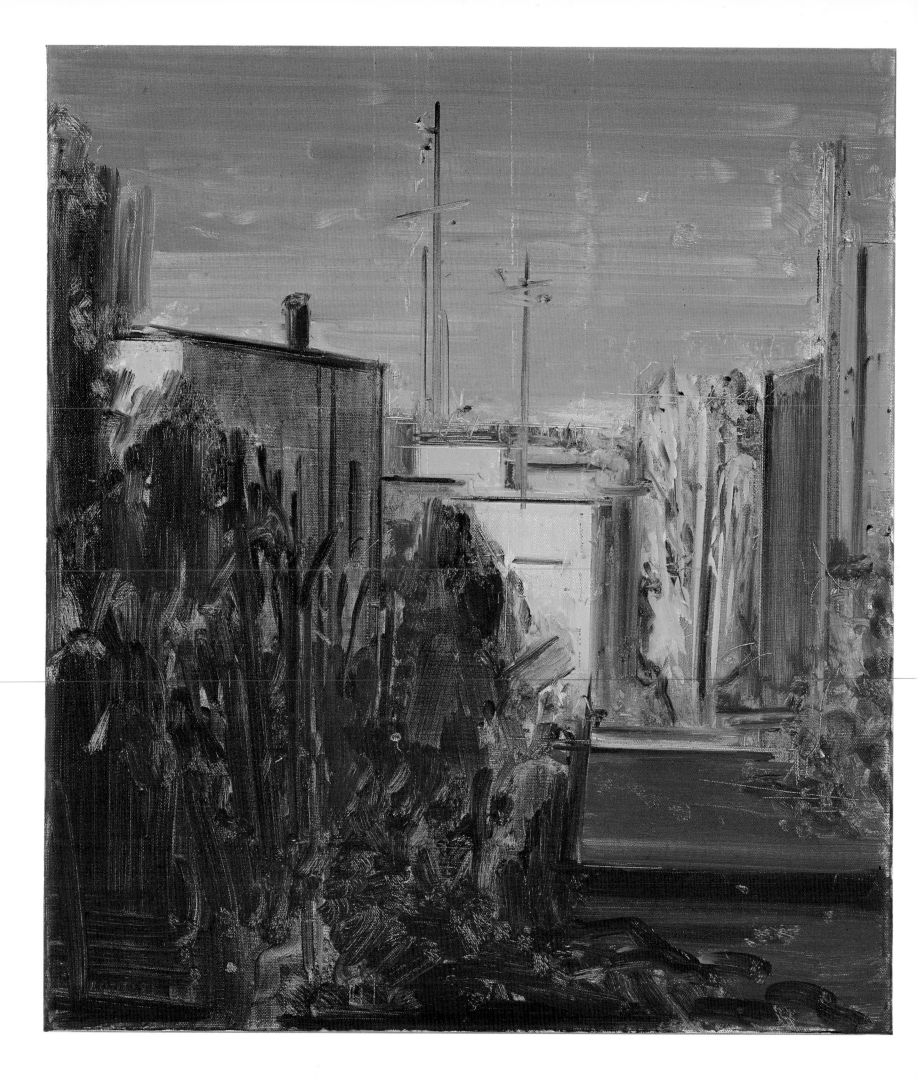

CHAPTER TWENTY-THREE

After the Six-Day War, my writing ground to a halt. What I wrote seemed pointless. I was working on the final draft of a novella, *Like the Apple of the Eye*. It was my first serious attempt to reconnect with my parents and grandparents, but all my efforts to concentrate and bring the novella to completion seemed to flounder. At that time, people's life stories were pouring out of the newspapers and the radio, and yet I felt myself outside of time and place.

Agnon, who usually did not pay much attention to those he was with, picked up on my distress and told me on one of our walks: "Heaven gives every creative person his own portion. The fortunate receive a portion of black earth that's easy to plow. Others get barren earth full of stones. Your lot is a not an easy one. But it's yours, and no one apart from you can work it."

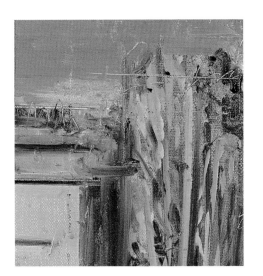

This egotistical and rather impenetrable man never failed to surprise me anew with his acute perceptions. In those days I would accompany him on his walks around Meah Shearim, Rehavia, and Sha'arei Hesed. In Meah Shearim, he would go from store to store, buying pamphlets and books. He always haggled, trying to get a bargain. I liked to hear him talk Yiddish. He spoke exactly like my grandfather, who had been born not far from the city where Agnon had been born.

It was in the alleyways of Meah Shearim that I saw Agnon's loyalty to his father and to the heritage of his forefathers. I sometimes had the feeling that everything he did and all his wanderings about the city were nothing but an ongoing search for a scrap of information that could throw light on some unknown angle of his hometown. Once he told me, "The city of my birth was full of amazingly wise men. Their lore was buried with them and it's up to me to find it and bring it to light. I'm not always as diligent about my work as I should be."

Agnon undoubtedly had in him something of the actor who will, by turns, dress in the rags of a pauper and the clothes of a king.

Despite all the external and internal pressures, on the whole I kept faith with my core and I wrote only about what I had experienced. I didn't stray into other pastures, though there were times when I was tempted to write historical short stories. I thought that the historical angle might deepen my writing. After the Six-Day War, I tried and failed again. It was then clear to me for once and for all that it was simply not in my power to write something outside my personal experience. Apparently, there are limits to the imagination. Writing about prophets or kings, or even the ordinary people during the Second Temple period would entail writing that had an ideological or didactic slant to it—and in the best instance that writing would be illustrative. It would be everything—except literature.

So if that were the case, why go out on a limb? How would I benefit from this distance from the literary point of view? People with ideological tendencies project themselves into different periods in order to clothe the characters that they have imagined and invested with their own ideas and thoughts. And there are those who liken themselves to prophets and to kings. The characters are marionettes in their hands. My search was, and still is, for living souls, and if possible for people like me—people whom I have been among, people like me. My characters are not weak people, but

Every few years I find myself a corner in a new café. After many years in one place, the eye grows weary, concentration diminishes and the place no longer yields up its melody. After Zauber's death, I abandoned Café Rehavia. When he was alive, it was a place that had inspired me, and after each time there, I would jot something down in my notebook. After his death, the place lost its magic.

neither can they pride themselves on daring feats or great wisdom. They have gone through hell and they emerged from it. That hell changed them and made them a little different from others. They spend their entire lives wondering how they should live and what they should do.

During that period, I would spend many evenings at Leib Rochman's house. It was more than a home for the Yiddish writers who flocked to him from all over the world. The Six-Day War had made the connection between the Jews of the Diaspora and Israel so much closer, yet despite the euphoria, the fate of Yiddish had already been sealed. Yiddish newspapers and publishing houses were steadily closing down, and with the death of each Yiddish writer or poet, the spiritual life of the language and its literature shrunk.

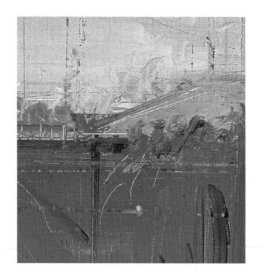

The leave-taking from Café Peter had been hard and slow. In 1968, we moved from our little apartment in Baka to Kiryat Moshe. The journey from Kiryat Moshe to the German Colony, which meant two buses, was long and tiring, but that wasn't the reason I ceased coming to Café Peter. My friend Tina, whose face I had gazed at for years, thirstily lapping up every word that she uttered, passed away. For years I had been spellbound by her and by the friends who surrounded her. After her death, it was as if darkness fell on all of us. She was fifty-three when she died. In my eyes she looked much younger: she illuminated the place with a wisdom that came from a body in constant pain. Suddenly, it was as if we had been orphaned from a young mother.

That was what was happening. But at Rochman's home, you'd encounter a kind of enthusiasm that was not of this world. The Prose and poetry would be read aloud into the early morning hours and the singing went on after midnight. Sometimes it seemed like a long funereal wake and sometimes like a desperate attempt to resurrect the dead. The flame of poetry would be stoked with strong coffee and cognac.

During the 1950s and 1960s I would go to lectures given by Dov Sadan, Martin Buber, Gershom Scholem, Yehezkel Kaufman, Shimon Halkin, Yeshayahu Tishby—each of them a giant in his own field. They enlarged my horizons, giving me new concepts, unfolding before my eyes the map of Jewish history and Jewish

These evenings would not always end quietly; sometimes there were outbursts. Most of the Yiddish writers had belonged to the *Bund* in their youth, or had been communists. The hidden feuds among those who took part in these *soirées* was longstanding and bitter, but for the most part, these fiery nights would draw to a close with slow partings and a quiet leave-taking.

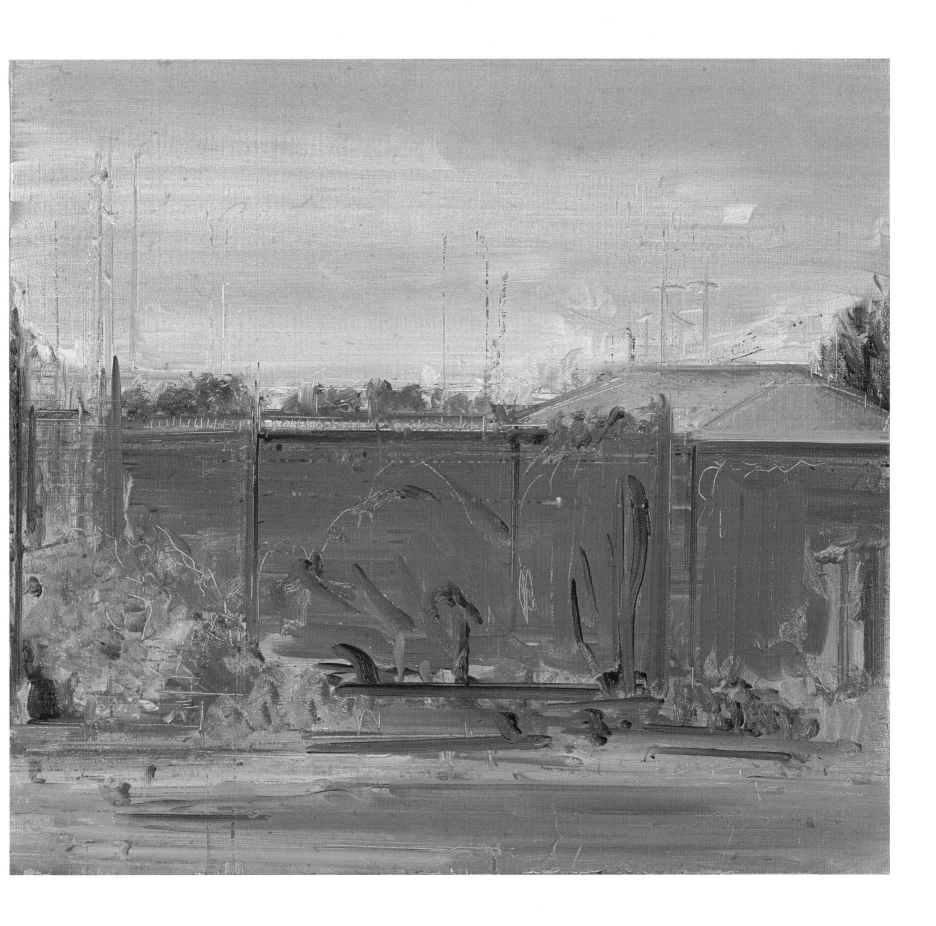

thought; however, I did not learn writing from them. Writing is something you learn from a place you are connected to, from people who reflect what you are. Tina and her Austro-Hungarian circle were my literary saloon. It was through them that I got to know myself and my parents. They embodied everything that was hidden in me and that I had been unaware of. They had *lived* the German of my parents, their assimilation, their distaste for any aspect of institutional Judaism; they had also been through the war and experienced all it had wrought in us. My childhood was dispersed over many places; in every café I discovered some long-lost part of myself. The moment I would discover people in a certain café who were from a place near where I had been born, or were close to my own heart, I would immediately begin going there regularly; sometimes for a couple of months, sometimes for years. That's how it happened with Café Peter and the other cafés.

There were many people whom I loved at Café Peter, but it was Tina who I loved more than anyone else. In her, I suppose, there must have been something of my mother, or of my mother's friends. Her broken body had not broken her. It was not only her extensive knowledge of pharmacology and medicine that she shared with people, but she also encouraged and gave them strength. With each person she found the reason that made it worthwhile for them to live. To me she said—indirectly—that a work of art that doesn't understand weakness, or lacks compassion and consolation—better it remain unwritten. We are alone in the world, and without love there is no reason to live. She, who was confined to a wheelchair for most of the day, taught her friends to be swift to offer help. She always knew how to make people happy with little gifts. She made her living by working in a pharmacy, and she would bring with her small vials of perfume, eau de Cologne or hand cream. Once she brought Big Arthur some soap. He was so moved by this that he took off the cap on his head, as if about to fall on his knees.

As I've said, I didn't exchange a word with Tina during the time I went to Café Peter, yet I had the feeling that part of what I was doing, perhaps the most meaningful part, was through her guidance or with her encouragement. Her death was a blow to us all. With Arthur it was quite visible. His large body seemed to sink down all at once. He spoke of the late Tina as if talking of a sister which death had snatched away.

One month after her death, her friends held a memorial gathering at the WIZO club house. The friends who had saved her in the war did not describe how they had rescued her but what she had meant to them. They also tried to make Arthur say something. He was embarrassed, imploring them to let him be. For some reason, the memorial service concluded with singing *Hatikvah*, the national anthem. Everyone wept, including me.

After her death, Tina's circle drifted apart. People continued to come to Café Peter, but not like before. Sometimes all of them would gather there, and for a moment it seemed as if the group was about to come back to life. But we were just fooling ourselves. We knew that without Tina, it was each of us for himself.

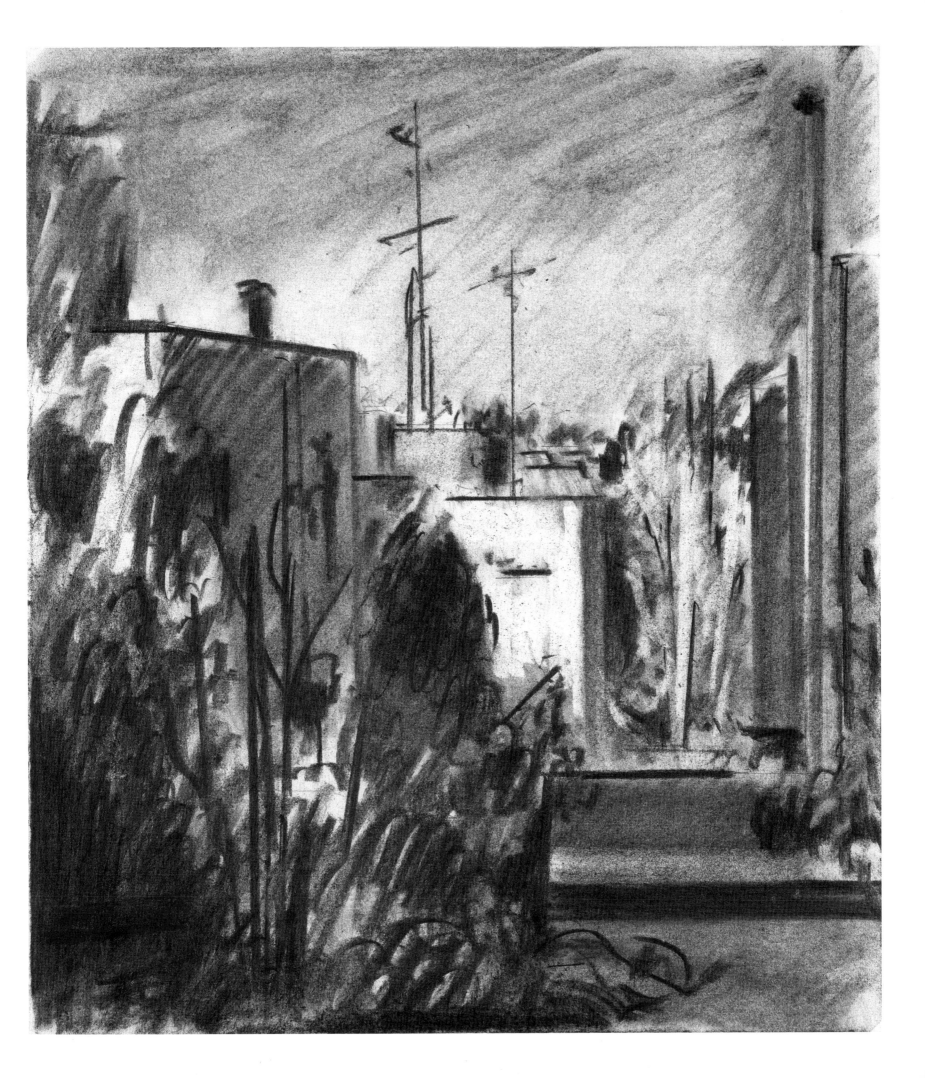

CHAPTER TWENTY-FIVE

In the mid-1960s and up till the 1970s, I would spend my time in Café Atara, on Ben Yehuda Street, which was a well-known meeting place for writers, journalists, painters, and professors. Occasionally, I would also drop into the Café Rondo in the Independence Park, and to Café Nava on Jaffa Street, but my regular place was Café Atara.

At Café Atara, in the heart of Ben Yehuda Street, time pulsed at an accelerated pace. Here newspapers passed from hand to hand, every news item had its interpreters and explainers. This place was permeated with the here-and-now in the full sense of the phrase. After years at Café Peter, life here seemed to be effervescing. At first this sense of over-brimming bothered me, but I quickly got used to it. By now, I was no longer in need of "models". The faces, the languages, the gestures, and the silences that I had absworbed at Café Peter, at Café Pat, and at Café Rehavia, were already part of me. I had but to link them to memory, to knead it carefully and then to allow the story to flow.

Agnon was astonished: "You write in Café Atara—in the midst of all that racket and confusion, with everyone looking at you?" He himself was a fanatic about quiet at home, and everyone was warned not to disturb him. I never made a fuss about my writing. Everything I wrote was in cafés, mostly quiet cafés, but also in bustling, crowded cafés. It never bothers me when people talk. Many writers have tortured their families because the noise made it difficult for them to concentrate. True, literary writing isn't regular writing, but then, neither is it a disease requiring the hushed silence of those around it. I have a great deal of respect for an artist who doesn't impose his moods on those around him. Writing is a struggle, and it should be between you and yourself, without involving additional people.

A close friend made this comment to me: "You're moving from café to café like you did in the war—from hiding place to hiding place."

I didn't like his comment, but I knew that there was some truth in what he said. To this very day I don't feel so comfortable in a rigidly orderly house, it makes me feel edgy. It is only in a café, among people, that I feel free. I suppose that I've brought those feelings with me from the years of the war, among other bad habits from "there": smoking, cognac, and coffee. It took me years to wean myself off them.

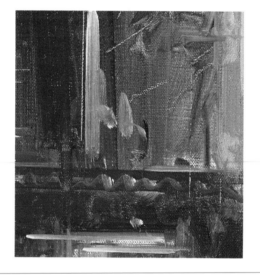

"One doesn't always have to explain to someone what he's doing," I responded to my friend.

"Ah, perhaps I was being naïve, but I thought that a writer should be conscious about what he does."

"Too much consciousness isn't necessarily a blessing. The blind flow that rises from the lines is the main thing. Revising, editing—these are products of the consciousness. They may be necessary, but this doesn't mean to say that they always improve the writing that has emerged from the unconscious."

⁊

The long short story and the novel are the forms that I like. In fact, to write a novel, and sometimes even a novella, means living a dou-

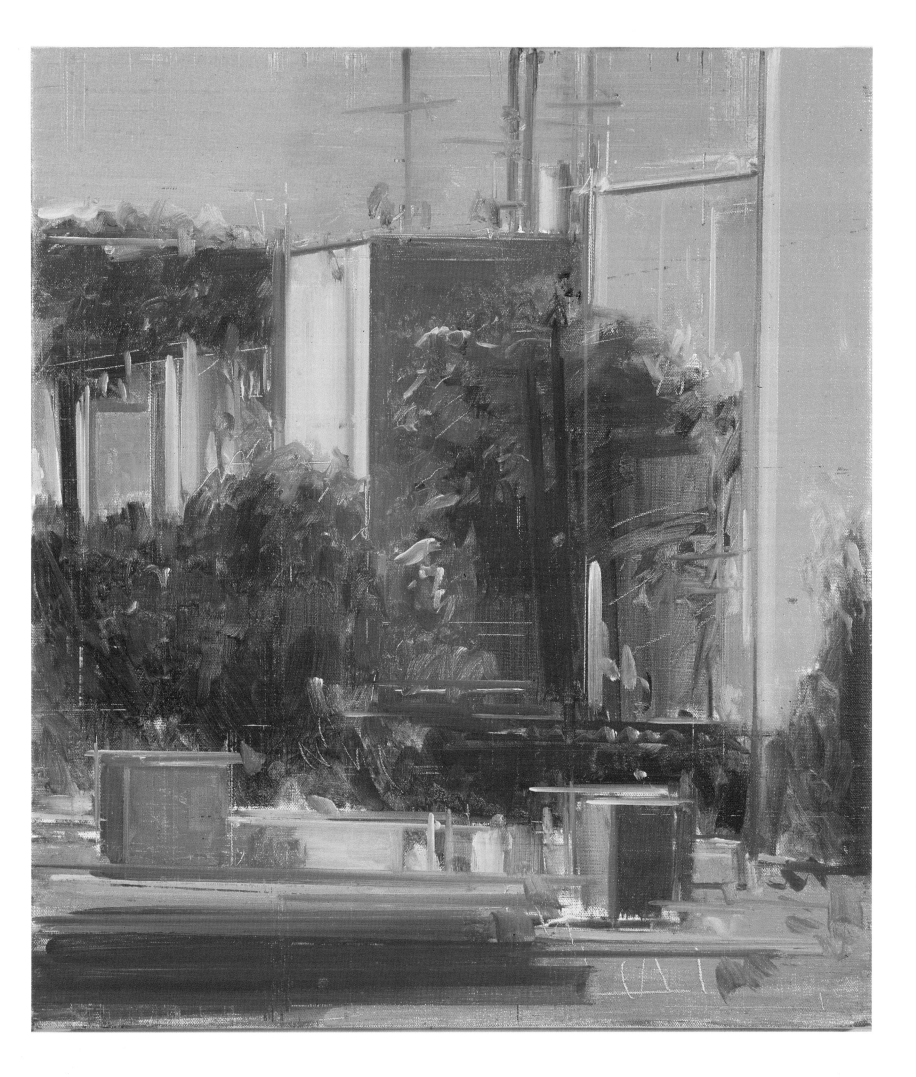

ble life for a year and a half or two. On one hand you lead a normal life, yet on the other, with the same intensity, you live another life in another place. For an author, this situation is something that is not mysterious but rather completely mundane. For years I struggled to make a living, which wiped out the most productive hours of my day. I would battle my tiredness by sipping coffee or having cognac. Writing is a huge effort. But unfortunately, even at my age, I cannot say that I've discovered the secret of writing. In writing, you are tested each time anew. A page where the words are set down on it right and flows—this is almost a miracle. When I finished the novella *Badenheim 1939*, I wept from sheer tiredness.

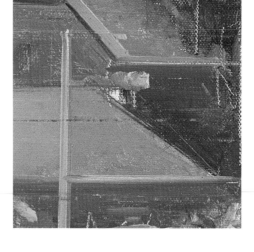

It didn't end there. When a few chapters of this novella were published in a literary magazine, a reader pounced on me in the café. He claimed that I was blaming the victims with blindness and with foolishness, and some day in the future, I would have to answer for it. It was useless trying to explain my position to him. He stood by what he had said. Sometimes it seems to me that in a country so awash with ideology, it's impossible to write literature. Life itself, in all its complexity, is not something we really ponder. Who are you? Are you with us or are you against us?

I hear this whenever I bring out a new book.

During the 1970s I would spend many hours in Meah Shearim. The thought that in Meah Shearim there were people whose lifestyle resembled that of my grandparents, pulled me to the neighborhood like a magic magnet. I would sometimes set out on these intense walks with either Agnon or Rochman, but quite often I went by myself. Agnon was rather stingy about sharing his impressions with others; he was also a detective in his own way, and he kept what he saw to himself. And yet, from time to time, he would share an observation about what people wore or perhaps the significance of a movement or a gesture that had escaped me. Rochman, on the other hand, was enthusiastic about everything he saw or heard in Meah Shearim. He knew each hasidic group's particular variations for prayer and Torah study, and he was familiar with every custom and its reason. Rochman's secular appearance in no way deterred the people of the neighborhood; they sensed that he was one of them. They felt they could both ask him and tell him things that are told only to someone you're close to.

It astonished me to what extent the people of Meah Shearim had recreated the life that Jews had lived in Europe. They also knew every small town, every *shtetl* where Jews had once lived; what branch of Hasidim there had been there, and why. They knew who the rabbi had been, who his faithful followers had been, as well as his opponents; they knew that rabbi's strengths and his weaknesses, and most important—they knew what his teachings had

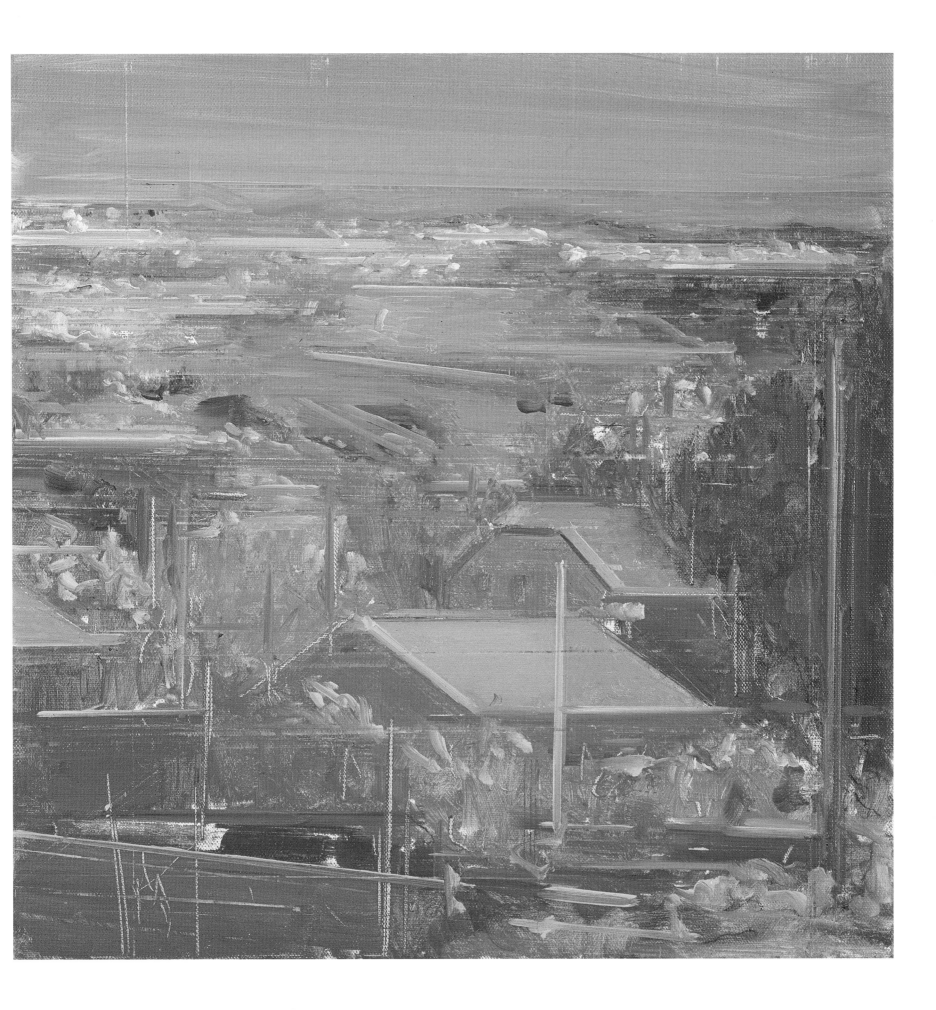

In a small town near Boston, there is a kind of "living museum" which has preserved the first houses of the Pilgrim Fathers. Men and women actors sit in these houses dressed in costumes that were worn at the time of the *Mayflower* and, in the language of those far-off days, tell stories about the lives and the experiences of the pioneers. They also answer visitors' questions. A tremendous effort has been invested in restoring the buildings and training the actors for their roles. Every year, thousands of visitors flock to this museum. We happen to have a living museum in the very heart of Jerusalem—but who goes there?

been and how they differed from the teachings of his opponents. Indirectly, Rochman taught me the way to talk with people who live in Meah Shearim, the way to ask and the way to interpret their answers. Religious people are not usually forthcoming when it comes to divulging information about their beliefs—usually they will only reveal things to those they feel they can trust.

My close friends would ask me repeatedly: What attracts you to Meah Shearim? Why do you spend so much time there? Most of my friends saw Judaism as an endless maze of coercion, superstition, backwardness, aggressiveness, and political extortion. They saw no redeeming qualities in the Jews of Meah Shearim—just annoying defects.

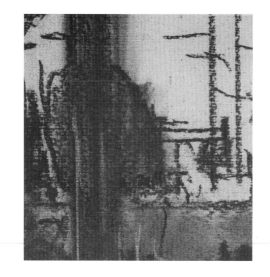

To return to my grandparents: we would travel to see them during the summer, and I spent some three or four summer vacations with them. It was during these trips, in the heart of the blue Carpathian Mountains, that I experienced a sense of mystery. Yet the way my grandparents worshipped was not strange. They were tall, sturdy people, who worked their land from dawn till dusk. On the Sabbath the men would wrap themselves in a *tallit*, pray and study.

In the Carpathian Mountains the trees were tall, but the houses and synagogues were low buildings. The synagogues had low entrances—a person would have to enter them almost bent over—and they were made of wood. The scent of pinewood would greet the worshippers, and it mingled with the smells of beeswax candles and dried flowers. In the Carpathians, people were great believers but used words sparingly; they tended to live long and when they died, it was usually in the fields, at work, and not in bed. As a child, I saw this clarity of life.

I did not defend them and did not renounce them. I simply tried to learn from them what I hadn't been able to learn in the university and from books. The way they held out against all progress, against the new State, against modernism—all that bothered me too. But I didn't pit myself against them; I didn't feel any superiority toward them. I had come to learn from them about belief, about prayer, about a religious routine and about an awakening from within; even about how they clung to their ancestors, and how they shielded themselves from modernity.

My parents did not see the wonders that I saw. They were not on easy terms with Jewish belief and only saw its defects. They

I neither wanted to live like them nor to resemble them. On the other hand, neither did I aspire to resemble my teachers, Gershom Scholem or Yeshayahu Tishby. Study for the sake of study held no interest for me—I wanted to live with my grandparents once again. On the few occasions that I had visited them in my childhood, I had seen a full and enchanting life, and it was this enchantment that I wanted to absorb.

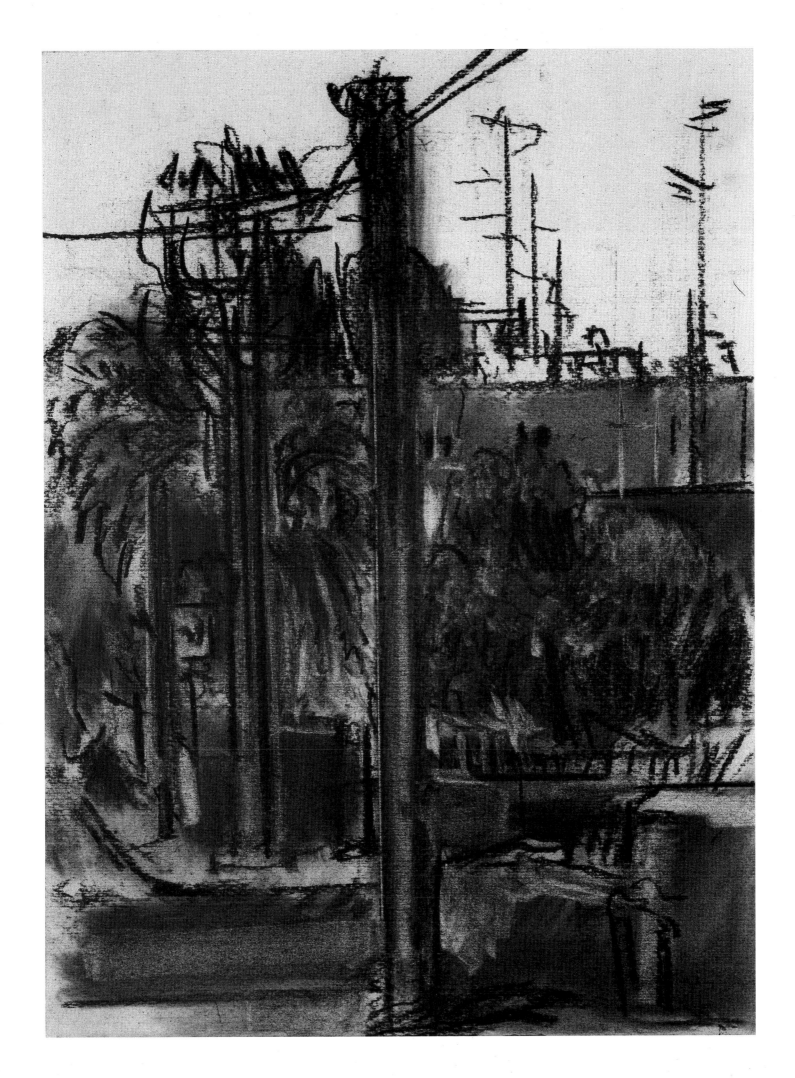

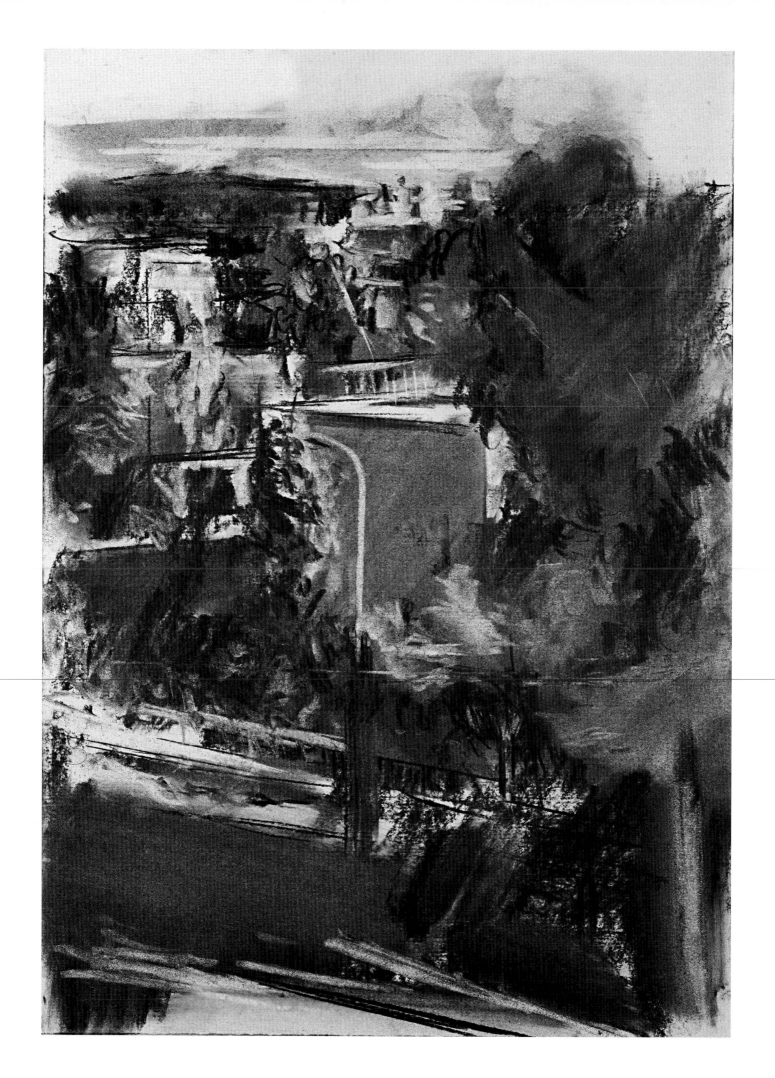

called the wonders "magic" or "superstition," and considered them a dangerous illusion or primitivism—beliefs held due to a lack of logic. After our vacation, they would do everything possible to uproot the visions of paradise from my soul. I, of course, refused, but they were more clever than me. They took me to the cinema, to the theater, to the museum, to the zoo and to toyshops—that's how they bribed me. When the war broke out I was seven. The fabric of our life was ripped to shreds. My mother was murdered and my father was taken from me. My childhood crumbled as if it had not existed. For years I neither saw my grandparents nor experienced the wonderful summers in which I had reveled in their presence. But one day, as if by chance, they were revealed to me as I was going up Agrippas Street on my way to the Mahaneh Yehudah market, and I knew then that the gates of light had been opened to me, and I saw what I hadn't seen all those years: hills and Jews are connected to one another and above, there's the sky's clear dome. And I knew then I was now permitted to enter those gates and write what the heart remembered and what the eyes had seen.

CHAPTER TWENTY-SEVEN

There is one café that has been erased from my memory, and not by accident. In the 1950s I would often drop by Café Vienna on Jaffa Street. It was a café with wide windows flooded with light, and by the standards of those times, it was grand and elegant. If my memory serves me correctly, there were even tablecloths. I've learned from experience that it is hard to concentrate in a café that is too public, or too brightly lit; far better to be somewhere with the light soft and dim.

The first time I went to Café Vienna I was with an extremely articulate young lady who was studying philosophy. We had both been attending Natan Rotenstreich's course in early philosophy. His lectures were complex and I had found it hard to follow his train of thought. Naturally, I blamed myself. But she—I've forgotten her name—had been delighted by his lecture. Her very satisfaction stirred up my ever-present sense of inferiority over my lack of education.

This was a time when I was impressed by people who had a way with words—and was convinced that if I could only learn to express myself, my thoughts would also be more lucid. I didn't yet know that silence is preferable to speech; that words may delineate the framework, but that artistic expression lies between the words—in the echo that the words evoke.

At the Hebrew University in the 1950s and 1960s there were army generals on leave and retired generals, kibbutz activists, and army officers who wanted to earn a degree. All of them were extremely well-trained public speakers; they knew what to ask and they knew how to answer. My education, or rather my lack of it, had schooled me in silence—it had given me practice in *not* talking. During the war I had learned to be suspicious, to be wary and to keep my distance from human beings. This turned me into a mute creature. Any time that I was asked something, the words would be stuck in my mouth. I would simply stutter my responses. If I had to give a talk, I would prepare it in writing; these talks were really more like reflections with myself than something for others.

In those days, it seemed to me that if I improved the way I spoke, the barrier that stood between myself and other people would be removed; I would be able to impress the young women with whom I studied, and even my writing, which had never flowed easily, would loosen up. Of course this was—whether I realized it or not—like declaring war on the habits I had acquired during the war. In fact, it was like declaring war on my own introverted character.

In order to remedy this, I enrolled in a course that Shlomo Morag was giving on public speaking. From the outset, it was clear to me that speaking to a group was not my strong point, and perhaps the best thing was to stay clear of the podium. However, in spite of myself, I was drawn to this delusion until it was my turn to speak. Morag, who was a sensitive man, saw how embarrassed I was and didn't put me to the test. He said something that made a great impression on me at the time: "Shy people can turn out to be excellent speakers; you mustn't lose hope." Yet clearly this rule did not apply to me.

At Café Vienna, I would sit at my regular place, gazing at people but not writing. I recall nothing that I wrote in the glare of that bright place. It was there that I would sometimes meet up with Haim Hazaz. He possessed a kind of sharp integrity. He read a few of my stories and liked them. His compliments were restrained, but not evasive. He advised me that the best thing to do was just keep writing.

At that time I was enthusiastically reading his book, *Mori Sa'id* ("Thou Who sits in the Gardens.") I liked the blend of daily life, mysticism and eroticism, but I could not have followed in his foot-

steps. I suppose that someone who has not studied Jewish thought from his youth would find it hard to follow his narrative. Students of the Talmud have always liked the writing of Hazaz, and some have even preferred it to the writing of Agnon.

I gave some of my stories to that highly articulate young lady with whom I had gone to hear the Natan Rotenstreich lectures, and asked her to read them. She prepared a list of comments for me: characters that needed fleshing out and that lacked ideas, the sketchy plot, anemic language…. It was evident that she had read the stories carefully. She had marked passages, jotted down questions and had dwelt on her reservations. I listened: her voice was assured, and her words sounded logical and correct. She touched upon the raw nerves of my weaknesses, or rather, what seemed to me to be my weaknesses at that time. Every word she said pierced me. Yet I was hurt that such a good-looking and intelligent young woman could find nothing positive in my writing. I tried to defend myself, but she had a single-minded determination, and for a moment it seemed to me that she wasn't talking to me but honing every word before it left her mouth.

I've met many people in the course of my life. There have been people who helped me to accentuate the good and the useful, and have helped bring out what was hidden inside me. However, in contrast to them, there were others who have just covered me with darkness, picked away at my soul, deepening my sense of inferiority and blocking my way. I ceased meeting up with that woman to whom words had come so easily, and also stopped going to Café Vienna. Apart from the sharp-angled face of Haim Hazaz, I can recall no other faces from there.

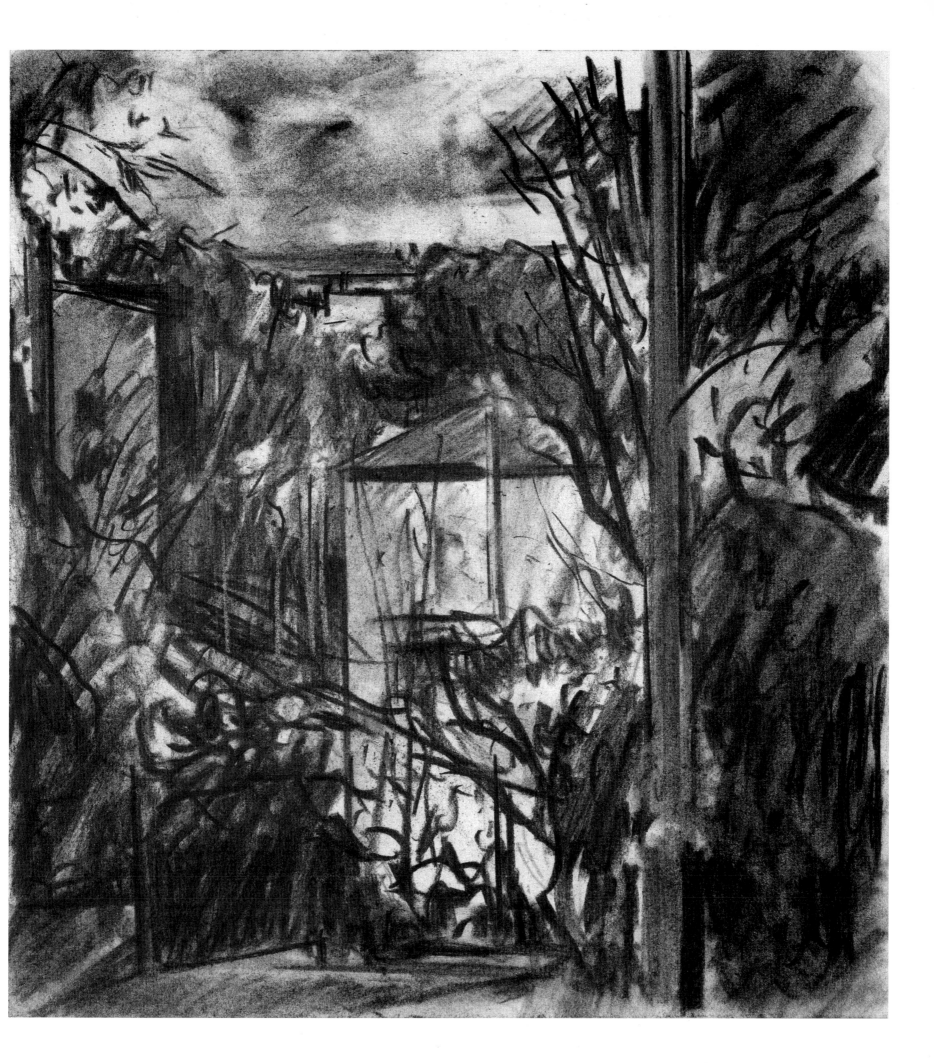

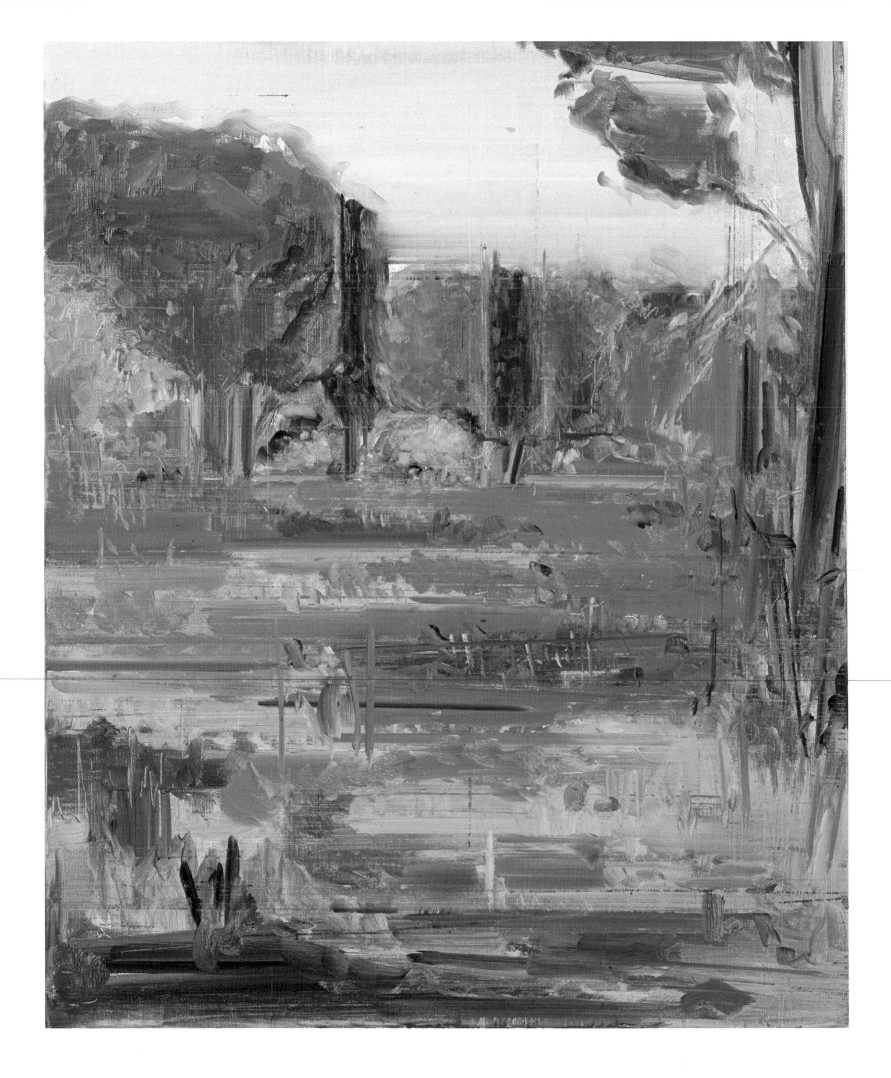

CHAPTER TWENTY-EIGHT

In 1972 my novella, *Like the Apple of the Eye*, was published. It was awarded the Brenner Prize. It was the first meaningful prize that I received. At the ceremony I said, among other things: "Agnon's artistic methods, and his overall content, are immeasurably richer in association, in his sources of language—than those of Yosef Haim Brenner. And when it comes to shades of feeling, half tones, the hues and the subtlest tones of hues, there is no doubt that Uri Nissan Gnessin surpasses Brenner in these respects as well. And if one takes the pedantry, the fine balance of what is said and what is left unsaid, it seems to me that even Gershon Schofman surpasses him. And despite this, none of them have what Brenner had. His weaknesses merge in such a way that they acquire a kind of power that elevates him to a different sphere, what I would call 'the sphere of religious pain.' One can admire Brenner, but it's impossible to follow in his footsteps unless you happen to be Brenner."

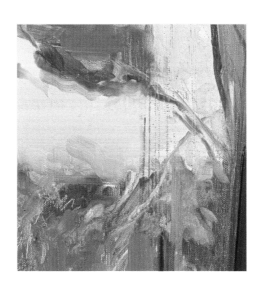

I had been an admirer of Brenner and I remained one, but beyond my admiration, I always felt a great closeness to him. It is widely known that he wandered from place to place before he came to Israel. His view of the world did not alter with all the turmoil around him. What he saw there, he saw here too. His literary outlook as a man of *belles lettres* was devoid of didacticism. The Jew, his existence, his character and fate—these had been the focus of his interest when he was in Europe and they remained so here. Not to mention his style, which also remained the same.

Upon arriving in Israel, most Hebrew writers changed their subject matter and even their style; but Brenner stayed Brenner.

Brenner lived in Jerusalem for some time, and I would imagine him coming out from one of the alleyways. Jerusalem suited him in a certain way; in this city in the twenties, ideologies jostled with each other. The city was more like one of the small towns from which he had come. Brenner did not believe that changing one's place meant changing one's destiny and I too, like him, do not believe it. In this sense, he was and has remained close to my heart.

I did not meet Brenner in Jerusalem, but I did receive an invitation from Rachel Yanait, who had been my director in the Youth Aliyah. She heard that I had been awarded the Brenner Prize and invited me to visit her. She had known Brenner well, but had no empathy for him. "He was always gloomy, sunk in his depression. He never saw any light on the horizon. He was discouraging…" That was her opinion. I listened to her, and said nothing.

We spoke about 1946, about the youth village for agricultural training in Jerusalem's north Talpiot neighborhood, and about child survivors, including myself. Her memory, it turned out, had not dimmed. She immediately reminded me that I had been a rather withdrawn child, that I was uncooperative and had rarely mingled with the others, and that I would sit reading books in German. She hadn't forgiven me these past sins. She herself had not changed. She held herself very erect and she was rigidly set in her ways. She had read two of my books. To judge from her expression, she was far from pleased, but she complimented me on my Hebrew.

Rachel Yanait had been quarried out of tough material: the Russian revolution and the Zionist revolution. Low-key literature, writing a Communist. Instead of us gathering here today in order to say something that will encourage him, look at how we're attacking him like beasts of prey. Appelfeld," he turned to me, "don't listen to them! You have to follow your own path and you mustn't be deflected from it. Because it's the right one."

His words moved me so much that I wept.

that did not bite into the meat of life, was not to her liking. She made no effort to hide her view that, at a time like this, literature should have a definitive message. I listened to what she said, but in my heart I was miles away. Memories of my time in the youth village came rushing back. And I felt sad thinking about those distant days when I suffered inwardly, but could not give it any expression.

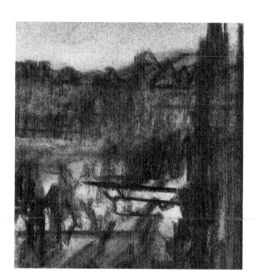

She asked me what I planned to do and I answered without hesitation, "To write."
"To write what?"
"To write whatever I'm supposed to write."
"And what about the will?"
"It doesn't intend to rebel against fate."
"*Ach*, Agnon, Agnon," she mocked as though she had caught me red-handed. She was, naturally, not among those who admired Agnon.

When we parted, she said to me: "I'm very proud of you. I'm sure that you'll develop and you'll write important things." When she said this to me, I suppose, what was before her eyes was not me and what I wrote, but what she hoped I would become: an author who would provide an example.

To celebrate my receiving the Brenner Prize, a group of writers and critics gathered at the home of Arieh Lipshitz to discuss my books. Most of them praised my earlier books more than my more recent ones. I did not feel comfortable and I didn't know what to say. Haim Hazaz, who was present at this gathering, stood up and raged like a lion against the critics. "Only someone deaf can't hear that Appelfeld has his own melody," he said. "He'll always write the same story; even if he writes about Alaska, it will always be about a restless Jew seeking to understand his character and his fate, and it makes not the slightest difference where that Jew happens to be. Appelfeld is not concerned with changes of locale, but with the eternal Jew, who may sometimes be a pious Jew and sometimes

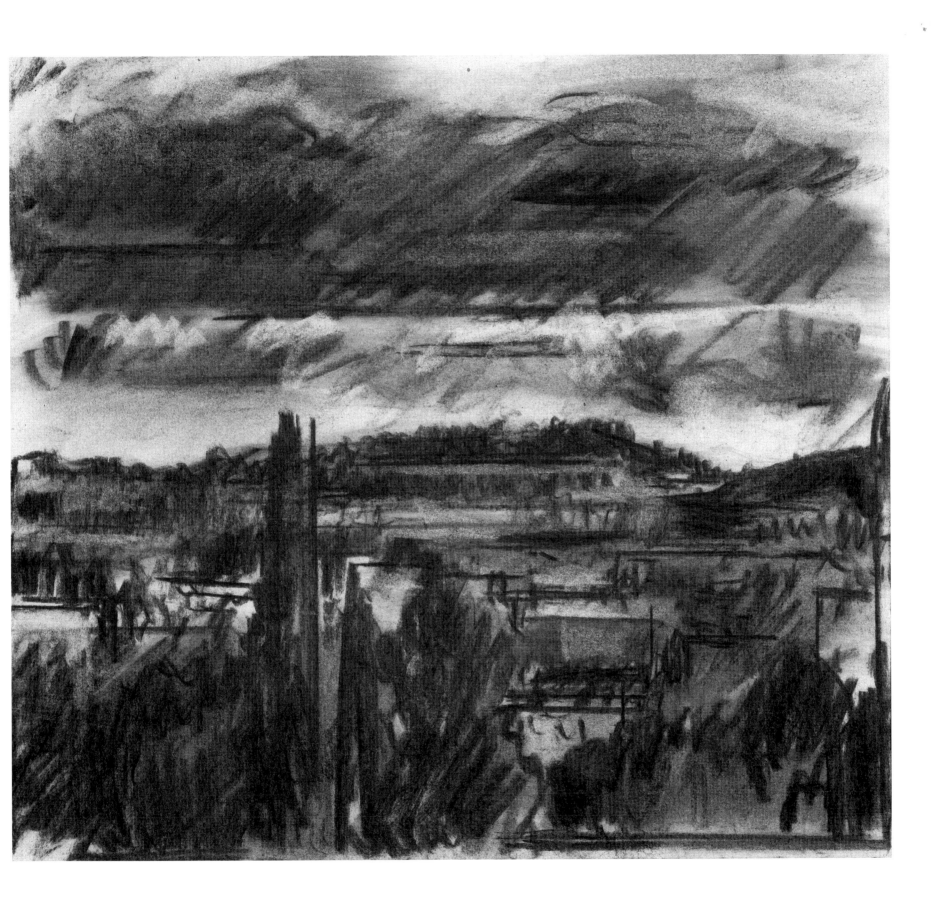

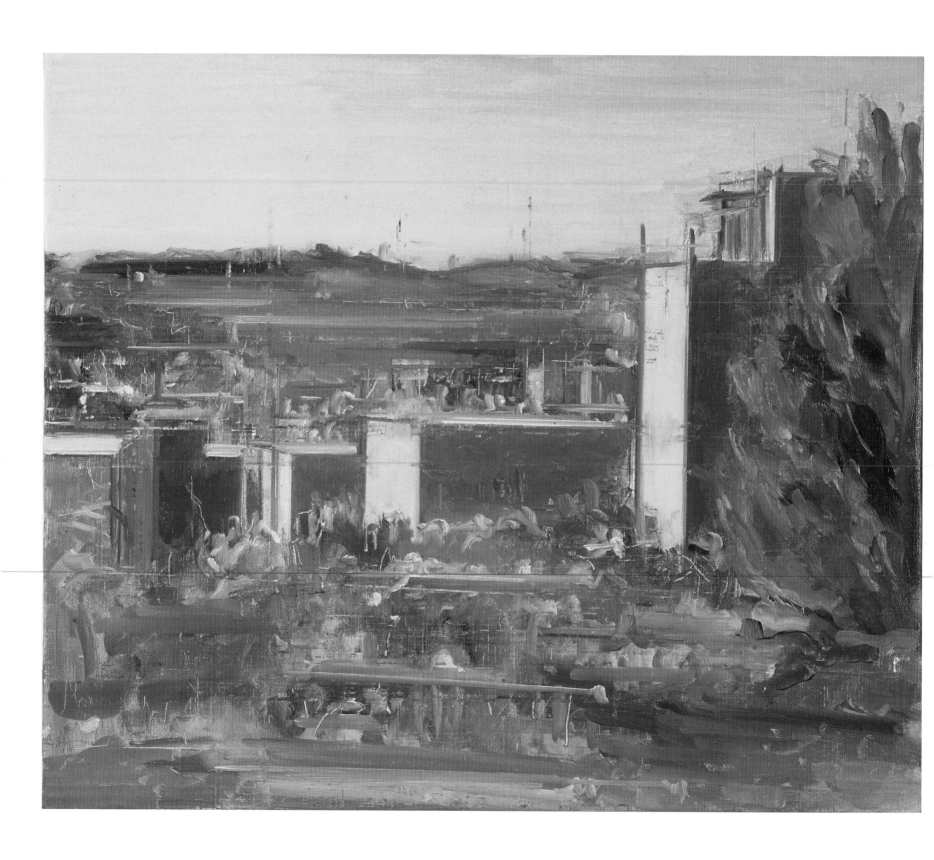

CHAPTER TWENTY-NINE

My friend P. comes to see me at Café Atara. We do our army reserve duty together. Born in Jerusalem, he's an architect. Unlike me, he went through elementary school and high school here, and has stayed on in Jerusalem, though the coastal plain is his real love. He thinks that Jerusalem is a miserable city, stifling, ugly. He won't go anywhere near Meah Shearim. Seven years younger than me, his parents were rescued at the last minute, but he feels no affinity for the place they have come from. He can hardly pronounce the name of the small town in which they were born. It's immediately obvious that he was brought up in a youth movement—he had a humanist upbringing with rational foundations, based on the Marxist doctrine.

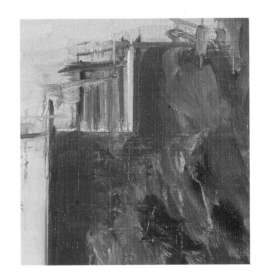

In his youth, P. read Freud on religion. He associates religion with the ultra-Orthodox, and has nothing positive to say about them. He calls them parasites. If it were up to him, he would have shut down all the religious institutions and conscripted all the *yeshiva* students into the army. He considers a Jewish education that doesn't include the study of science limited, dangerous; *yeshiva* students should be forced to learn science and take classes in democracy.

"And wouldn't this entail a certain amount of coercion?" I ask carefully.
"It would, but it's necessary both for them and for us."

It's hard to argue with beliefs. P.'s relationship with people who have survived the Holocaust is also critical: they're too immersed in their past. Even his own parents, who were saved at the last minute, never cease speaking about their home town. He thinks that the Holocaust stirs up dormant religious feelings in survivors. The survivors, in their wish to identify with the victims, are liable to fall back on the beliefs of their forefathers; anyone religious is, in the final analysis, nationalistic.

I keep my opinions to myself and prefer to listen. And for a moment it seems to me that he isn't from here. In my childhood I would often hear words like "sorcery", "fetishism", "anachronism". For some reason it seemed to me that the Holocaust might have changed this over-confident frame of mind, and yet it didn't. My friend speaks the way people spoke then.

And what does he think of people like Yeshayahu Leibowitz, Hugo Bergman, or Martin Buber? He says he agrees with their political stance, but their religiousness is beyond the pale. Beneath his words, I sense an oblique criticism of my books, and it turned out that I was not far off the mark. He has discerned that I do have empathy for people who have some attachment to religion. This, in his opinion, is a defect that I should really try to correct one of these days, but as for my relationship to the Holocaust—there it's doubtful that I'll be able to change. I am too immersed in that time. It is impossible to live a normal life with such a chip on one's shoulder. Memories such as these are a useless burden. Instead of helping people to move away from this trauma, what I'm doing is encouraging their preoccupation in it.

Again, in his voice, I heard those voices from my childhood…. My uncle was a Communist to his very marrow, and I clearly recall the discussions in the evenings that took place in the house, even though I didn't understand them at the time. For years I would carry them around inside me like a sweet secret. Because of this secret, I listen very attentively to my friend's words. He's so wrapped up in himself; it's hard for him to understand my relation to belief and people who believe. You won't find any sense of aesthetics among them. In their neighborhoods, you won't find a park worthy of the name, nor a pleasant building. Not even a corner to sit down. The *yeshivas* look more like warehouses than places for human beings. Immigrants who came from Central Europe attempted to change the character of the city, they built the neighborhoods of Rehavia, Beit Hakerem, and Talpiot, and they hoped that in Jerusalem the European and the Mediterranean styles would mingle. However, the religious public, with its birthrate steadily on the rise, has changed this trend. They've brought the ghetto into the city. And not only did they bring it with them, but they intend to impose this way of life on everyone. In another generation or two—according to his forecast—his Jerusalem would be one large ghetto where someone secular would feel like a complete stranger.

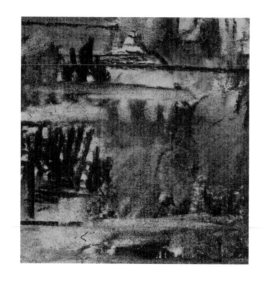

Anyone who has been brought up in the secular youth movements has a contemptuous attitude toward metaphysical thinking. My friend loves the sea, he loves certain places in the Galilee, tennis, Mediterranean food, and trips abroad. Any time that the word "Jew" pops up, he shrinks. In many ways, that's the Zionist dream. Who does not remember that magic word: "normality"? Is it really a product of this dream? Jewish complexity is beyond him. My friend refuses to accept it, just as he refuses to accept his parents' feelings toward their little town that was completely destroyed. In his opinion, Jerusalem should be filled with public gardens and parks, and not with *yeshiva* academies.

P. is beside himself at the thought that the religious population has increased, devouring neighborhood after neighborhood. I am sorry that he feels no closeness to the city that he was born in, neither to his parents, nor to what they went through—to say nothing of Jewish history and belief. He's a man who's open to music, to literature, theater, but he spurns anything to do with Jews or Judaism. He will travel thousands of miles to see a scenic church built on the edge of a cliff, or a temple in Mexico, but he won't enter a synagogue in Jerusalem's Sha'arei Hesed neighborhood. Sometimes it seems as if he's a true son of the assimilated Jews from the city of my birth. They also felt revulsion to anything Jewish. The Communists in my town would make a bonfire every Yom Kippur just to show everyone that they had immolated all connection to the faith of their fathers.

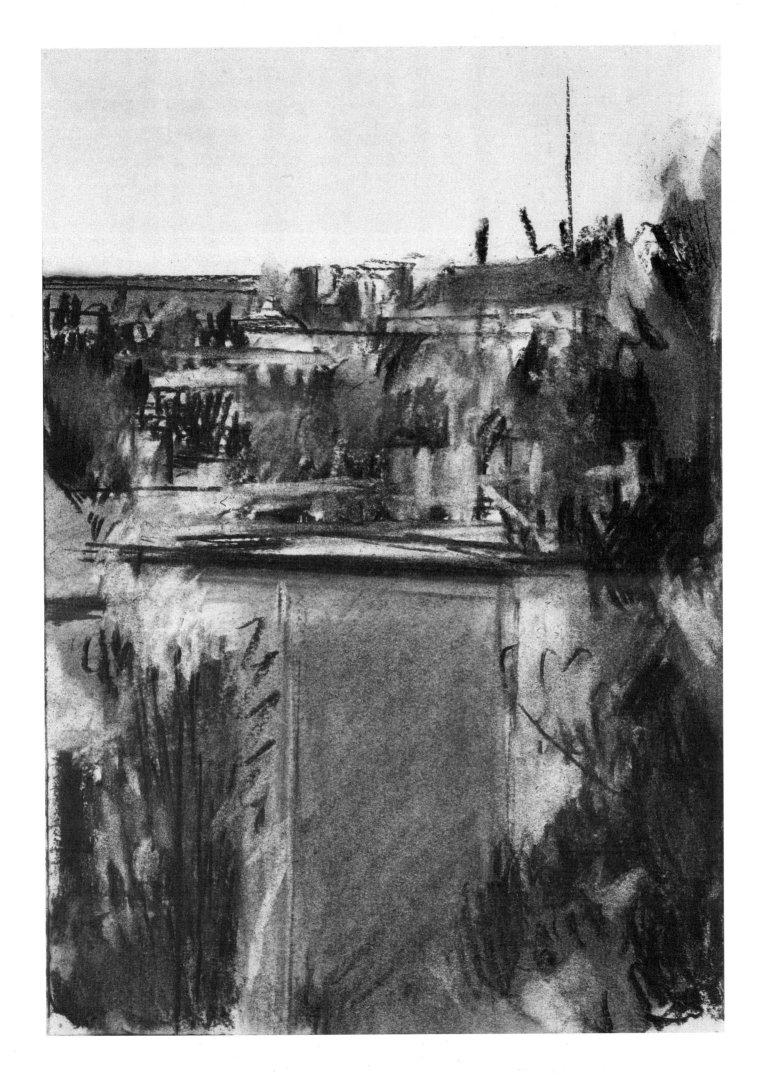

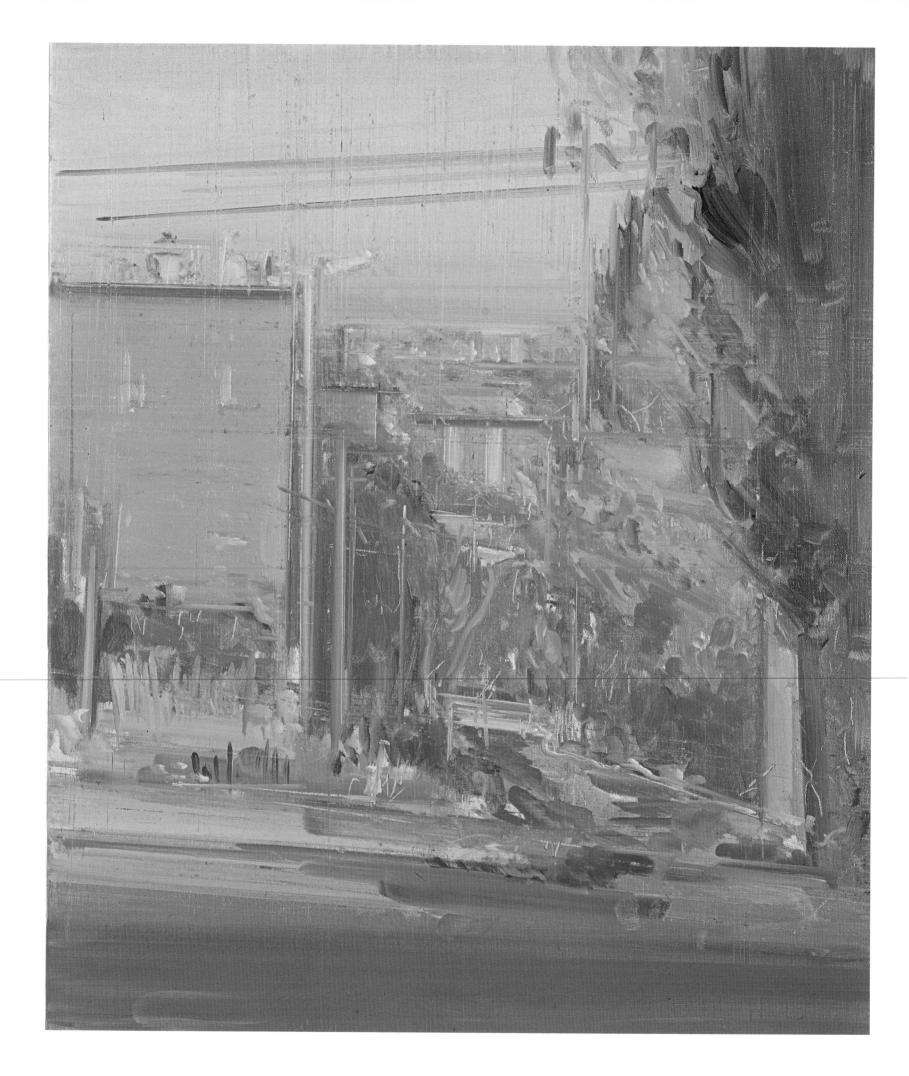

CHAPTER THIRTY

In January 1973, Brother Raphael, a Roman Catholic, who had read some of the stories that I've written that were set in Italy—requested an interview with me. My immediate, instinctive, feeling was to reject his request. I was certain that he'd be probing my opinion on politics or religion. I don't like to pontificate. In my experience, religious or political beliefs cannot be changed; arguments only sharpen the existing differences, and no good ever comes out of these discussions.

I expressed my reservations to Brother Raphael. He immediately responded by saying that this would absolutely not be an interview on political issues or matters of belief. He was interested in talking to me about Jews, about their fate in Europe and their ingathering to the land of their forefathers. His voice, more than what he said, persuaded me. I agreed and we fixed a date.

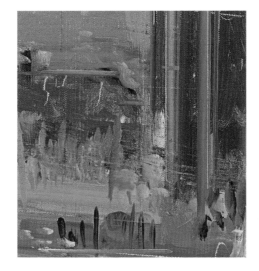

Brother Raphael had been living in Jerusalem for two years. He spoke Hebrew, and was knowledgeable in the ancient Jewish sources and in Jewish works of recent generations. A tall man, he was open and his voice pleasant. I saw that he was not a political man in the narrow sense of this concept.

"Where is your homeland?" was his first question.

The question, if truth be told, astounded and somewhat embarrassed me. I don't recall when and in what circumstances I had used the word "homeland". Perhaps never. My grandfather and my father had also never called the country where they had been born "a homeland". True, my parents did love their city and the Carpathian hills that surrounded them. My forefathers had lived in the area for some two hundred years, but it was not their homeland. That was in relation to "there". And as for "here"—from a formal viewpoint, of course Israel is my homeland, but quite honestly, I'm not sure if my affinity to Israel is the attachment of a native child to the place of his birth. It's hard to call a land where you haven't grown up a "homeland". The word "homeland" indicates living somewhere continuously, and it's a very intimate relation. That and more: the word "homeland" was used by the Nazis, beyond it's normal meaning, as a word by which to indicate sole ownership. In other words, the homeland belonged to the Germans and not to the foreigners.

"I prefer to use a simpler word—'home'. My answer to your question is that my home is here."

"Would it be true to say that your relation to Israel is the relation of a traditional Jew? In other words, a kind of impermanent state. In your Italian stories, after the Holocaust, Jews continue to wander from place to place. They don't hurry to get to Israel—in fact, they're afraid of the journey. Am I wrong?"

"I'll try to answer. Up to the age of fourteen, I was forced to wander about the world. I've been here since 1946. I was a farmer, I served in the army, I studied at the university, I started a family. I'm bound up in this place, involved in it. But did I cut myself off from the places where my forefathers lived? Definitely not. It's hard to uproot from the heart the land in which your forefathers lived for hundreds of years. Those distant places, even though I left them at a young age and in very extreme circumstances, be-

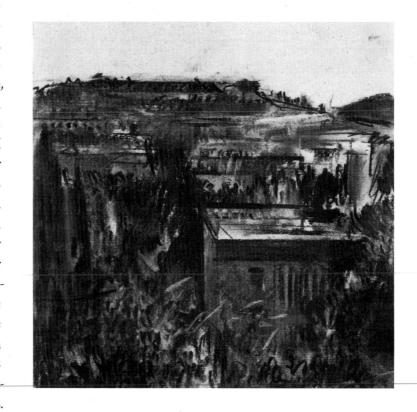

came part of my very being. I sometimes find myself yearning for those seasons of the year, for the houses in which my grandparents used to live, for the synagogue and for the cemetery. I long for the Jews and all that they did there, tangibly and in spirit. I was born in the Carpathian Mountains, the birthplace of the Ba'al Shem Tov. I only discovered this here, but ever since I've known it, I've been his follower in heart and in soul. And as for the restless wanderings: in the Holocaust, and immediately after it too, every Jewish survivor felt as if the ground was burning beneath his feet. After the Holocaust there was a deep desire among the refugees to flee from themselves and to disappear as Jews. Coming to Israel was a certain kind of return to Jewishness. Hence the fear."

"Let's set aside the word 'homeland' and lets talk about the homes. Are the homes you talk about equally important?"

"Every home has its unique value. It's a matter of perception. I've mentioned the Ba'al Shem Tov and the Carpathians. I'm no less linked to Jews such as Kafka, Franz Werfel, Paul Celan—all of them came from the region that I came from. They nourish my soul with a different kind of Jewish food. Through the Ba'al Shem Tov I'm linked to my forefathers and to their beliefs, while Kafka has taught me to see myself in the context of the modern world. It's no coincidence that I mention Kafka. His three sisters were exterminated in the Holocaust."

"Is your relationship with Jerusalem a nationalistic or a religious one?"

"That, too, is a question that's not easy to answer. So as to avoid any misunderstandings, let me say straight out that I don't see myself as secular. Religious thought and feeling are not foreign to me. For years I studied Jewish thought, and continue to do so. But keeping the commandments—that's a level I have not attained. I don't belong to an observant congregation, and only attend synagogue infrequently. I suppose that a man who keeps the full tradition would call me, quite rightly, 'a secular Jew.' The word 'nationalistic' is not a word that I have use for. Throughout history, Jews didn't have any use for it. By the way, the word 'religion,' that, too, is not a Hebrew word; it has come to us from the Persian. I always identify myself as a Jew. The word 'Jew' means, in common usage, to be a *mensch*. This description suits me more than the description 'Hebrew' or 'Israeli.'"

"And yet still, you do have, if I'm not mistaken, a religious affinity to the city?"

"You've certainly observed that the word 'religious,' like the words 'homeland,' or 'Jerusalem,' are not easy for me. Not because I'm lacking a relationship to these words, but because of the clichés and pomposity that surround them. The very word 'Jerusalem' has already been choked up with lofty words. I find it difficult to speak of words and concepts without reexamining them. This scrutiny is sometimes the central focus, and not the final definition. It seems to me that one should speak about religious feelings not in bombastic, amused tones but in wary half-tones. My religiousness did not come from a communal religious life, but out of my own experiences: my brief visits with my grandparents in the Carpathians, my loneliness in the forest during the war, the light-filled skies of Jerusalem, the blue of the hills of Moab toward evening…. Those are extremely personal feelings, to which I added a certain amount of knowledge in the course of time. Its doubtful I could convey them to another person."

"Do you view the Jews' return to their homeland as the fulfillment of God's promise?"

"I can't claim to have thoughts of this height—I can't pretend to understand God's thoughts. I can imagine that a religious man might have such a thought. In his day, Theodor Herzl said that the return of the Jews to their land would be their return to Judaism. This approach is more understandable to me, and I feel that beyond this wishful thinking there is a certain truth in Herzl's statement."

"What do you have to say about the relationship of Christianity to the Jews?"

"This is not a question that should be put to me. From the very outset, Christianity had a negative attitude to Jews and to the

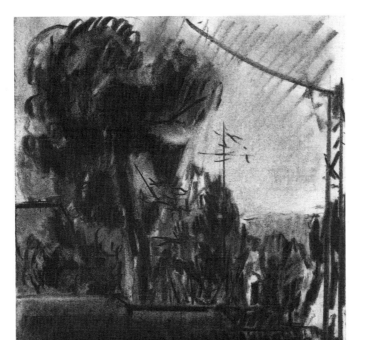

Jewish faith. This negativity only deepened with the years and it's well known how it assumed various faces and forms. It filtered down from the priesthood to the common people. Jews were perceived as the murderers of God, not as an allegory, but quite literally. This was mainly expressed in the image of Jesus crucified on the cross. Every believing Christian sees this before him every week in church. That, it seems to me, is a fair summary of the relationship between Christianity and the Jews. Because this was one-sided, since the Jews in this narrative played a passive role, it's hard for me to say anything. Christianity, it seems to me, has to face up to this."

"Are you angry at Christianity?"

"I do not feel anger at abstract things. There were Christians who took me into their home during the war and helped me, and there were those who put obstacles in my path. Once I heard a Ukrainian peasant woman saying to herself, 'If the Jews hadn't murdered Jesus, our Jesus would still be alive.' Of course she did not realize that I was a Jewish child. Imagine what would have happened had she known."

This interview, like the interviews before it, left me uneasy, but afterward I was happy that I had weighed my words, that I hadn't come out with anything that was not part of me, and that I did not say anything that I did not believe in.

CHAPTER THIRTY-ONE

The Yom Kippur War, like the Six-Day War, brought to the surface words and comparisons with the Holocaust. If the truth be told, whenever we face a great threat, the specter of the Holocaust looms.

When war broke out I was called up, though this time not as a rank-and-file soldier but as a lecturer, and I was immediately sent to the Suez Canal. During the long waits, amid the sand and the anxiety, I had plenty of free time to talk with the soldiers and the young officers, many of whom were sons of Holocaust survivors. I immediately noticed that the majority of them did not know one word of Yiddish. Yiddish had been the secret language at home. Parents had not bothered to teach their children this language—their mother tongue—nor anything about the beliefs of their forefathers. Neither did they tell them about what had happened to them in the ghetto and in the camps. In fact, they had hidden their lives from their children and had molded (albeit unintentionally) a life devoid of the thread of family history and without a spark of belief.

"Where are your parents from?" I asked.
"Poland."
"From which town?"
"I don't know."
"What camp were they in?"
"I don't know."
"What did they tell you?"
"They didn't."

That was more or less what I asked, and that was basically what they answered. The personal experience of the Holocaust had been kept from these youngsters. But as they spoke, I recognized expressions and gestures from their parents. There was no doubt they were connected to them, though it wasn't an inner connection.

The conversations brought up words like "ghetto", "camp" or the standard pictures of the Holocaust as they had been regurgitated so often in primary schools and high schools. For the most part, the associations that accompanied the words were negative or unpleasant or general, or distanced or even banal. For a moment I forgot that for years we had been nurtured on negative connotations to "there". Survivors internalized this and passed it on to their children. Now I could see what had been passed on, how it had been passed on, and what this process of transmission had done to the soul.

On the eve of the Yom Kippur War, I was interviewed by a young German journalist. He told me that his father had been a soldier in the Second World War, had served on the eastern front, and was then wounded and taken prisoner. I asked him if his father had told him something about the war.
"Nothing."
"And you didn't ask him?"
"I asked him, but he refused to answer."
"You don't know anything?"
"Nothing."
It was obvious that the young man was telling the truth.

An aggressor prefers to keep quiet and not to speak—that's understandable. But why should the victim also be preoccupied with repressing memories and trying to forget what happened to him?

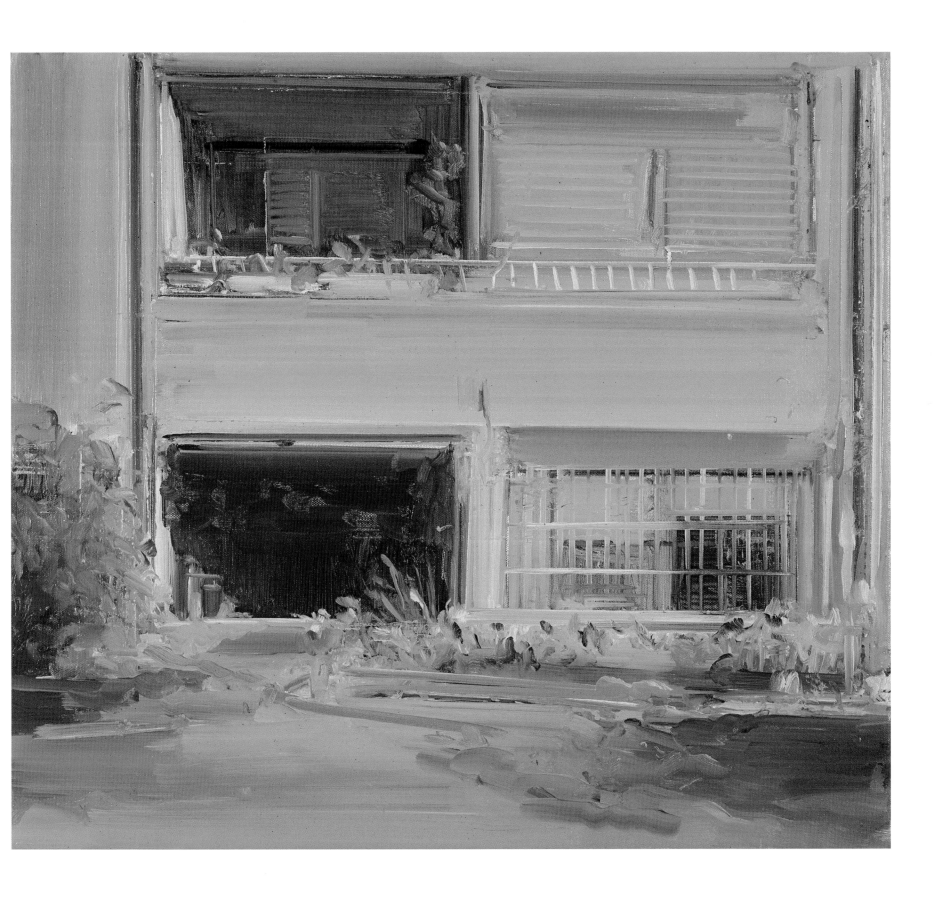

CHAPTER THIRTY-TWO

Upon my release from the army, I returned to my regular spot at the café. I didn't know where to start. It was as if all that had bound me to the past and to this place had been severed. I leafed through my papers and I felt lost. I wasn't the only one in such confusion. There was fresh bereavement on every street corner, and to deal with art suddenly seemed strange and irrelevant.

After a few conversations with the Israeli soldiers, I decided to make use of the texts that I had brought with me—some of Kafka's aphorisms, some excerpts from *Midrash*, some modern poems and a few meditations of Rabbi Nachman of Bratzlav. I had no idea what the reaction to these texts would be, but it was quite amazing. If beforehand the conversations had been somewhat superficial and had tended toward the subjective mood, when we now looked at the printed text, it forced us to work at a single word, a phrase, or individual sentence. A text that contains a certain truth stirs a person to even clearer thinking. It turned out that the soldiers—most of them high school graduates—were not really as detached from literature and from reflection as they seemed. In the prolonged waiting period, between one military exercise and the next, interesting ideas were exchanged, distinctions made, and things were brought up both from the heart and from life experience.

I was at the Suez Canal for about three months. It has often been said that we were caught unawares during the Yom Kippur War. I did feel that something internal really was shaken up, but it was hard to put one's finger on it. For religious soldiers, religion became more internalized. And among the secular soldiers, words from the soul seemed to surface. One evening, a soldier showed me two poems he'd written. Though slightly sentimental, and with some excess words in places, I immediately felt that this young man not only had a feeling for poetry, but also an understanding of the craftsmanship involved in this form.

I went back to teaching; in the evenings I would drift through Meah Shearim, Rehavia, and Sha'arei Hesed. When I write, I feel anchored to a time and a place; but when the writing no longer flows, it is as if a cloud descends and my world darkens and narrows.

After the Yom Kippur War the cracks in society started to show. The "Israel" myth, on which two generations had already been raised, seemed to lose its relevance and meaning. Following the war, the protests and the demonstrations were sporadic and unfocused—more indicative of distress than striking at a clearly defined targets.

My internal world had also been shaken. In the days before the Yom Kippur War, my writing had flowed fast. Past and present seemed to merge together, and I was sure that there was nothing like this city for reconciling contrasts; yet suddenly it was as if the ground under my feet had been swept away.

I was again approached by a newspaper which tried to lure me into

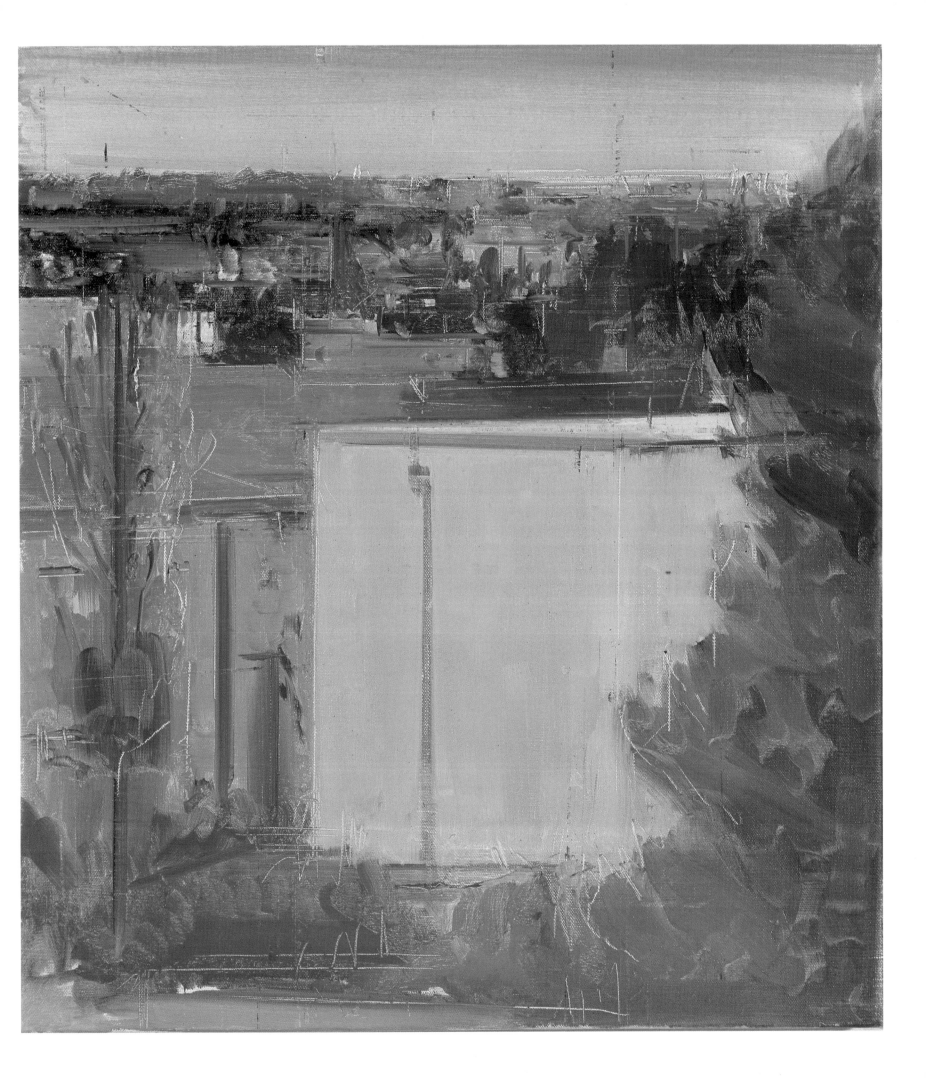

that I was telling them a tale. I went from the lighter to the heavier; from the end, from the forest.

"And weren't you afraid at night?" I was asked, the childrens' eyes full of wonder.
"I was afraid."
"And how did you overcome the fear?"
"I thought about my father and my mother."
"And that helped you?"
"Yes."

Of course I didn't tell them about the Ukrainian peasant who had chased me and who had thrown his ax at me, and how I was only saved by a miracle, nor about the hunger that so tormented me until I finally sank into hallucinations from which I could barely awaken. Neither did I tell about the vomiting and the diarrhea, the way my knees trembled, nor the headaches, and not about being terrified of the trees and the shadows and of the birds of prey which tear the night with their cries. I told them about the fruit that I found in the forest, and about the water from the stream that I subsisted upon.

"Dad, are you telling us everything?" They were suspicious.

"As much as possible."

It was then that I knew that there were sights and things that I would never tell, not even to myself. They were so divorced from all common sense, so un-*believable* and so terrifying, that it was better not to talk about them. Any mention of them was liable to make an unbelievable legend of terror out of the Holocaust, or even worse—a fabrication.

writing a weekly column. Again, the same well-worn argument: a writer should be involved, journalistic writing is no less vital than literature, journalistic writing will bring you readers. My writing had come up against a dead end, and I was tempted. This time, however, what saved me was not clear-headedness, but rather my own stubbornness, and I turned the offer down.

On my return from the war I saw how much my children had grown. The first-born, Meir, was eight years old, and the younger son, Itzhak, was five. They had absorbed much of what had been happening. On our outings in the afternoons, especially on Saturdays, we would have long conversations. I was sorry that I didn't know how to play with them at the playground or on the grass. At the outset of the Second World War, I had been seven, and I was immediately thrown into the hardships of the ghetto and of the camp. Throughout the entire war, until I came to Israel, my life resembled that of a small animal fleeing from its hunters. When I came to Israel, at the age of fourteen, I already felt like a grownup. The impulse to play, which every young person has, was gone. While those of my age played around, I would stand on the sidelines, watching them in wonder.

Up till the Yom Kippur War I generally didn't talk with my children about the Holocaust. Every time I wanted to tell them something, it was as if the words were swallowed up in my mouth. Yet now it was as if my encounter with the soldiers at the Suez Canal opened my own mouth, and I hoped that from now on I would be able to tell them things. Unfortunately, however, the story of my childhood during the war is not exactly a fairly tale.

Yet to my surprise, my children knew more than I imagined. At home they'd absorbed words, half sentences, and stories that I had told friends late at night. They knew that my mother had been murdered at the beginning of the war, that I had lived in a ghetto and in a camp, and that I had escaped to the forests. When I began to talk to them, I felt immediately that if I told them details about the atrocities, they wouldn't believe me. At best, they would think

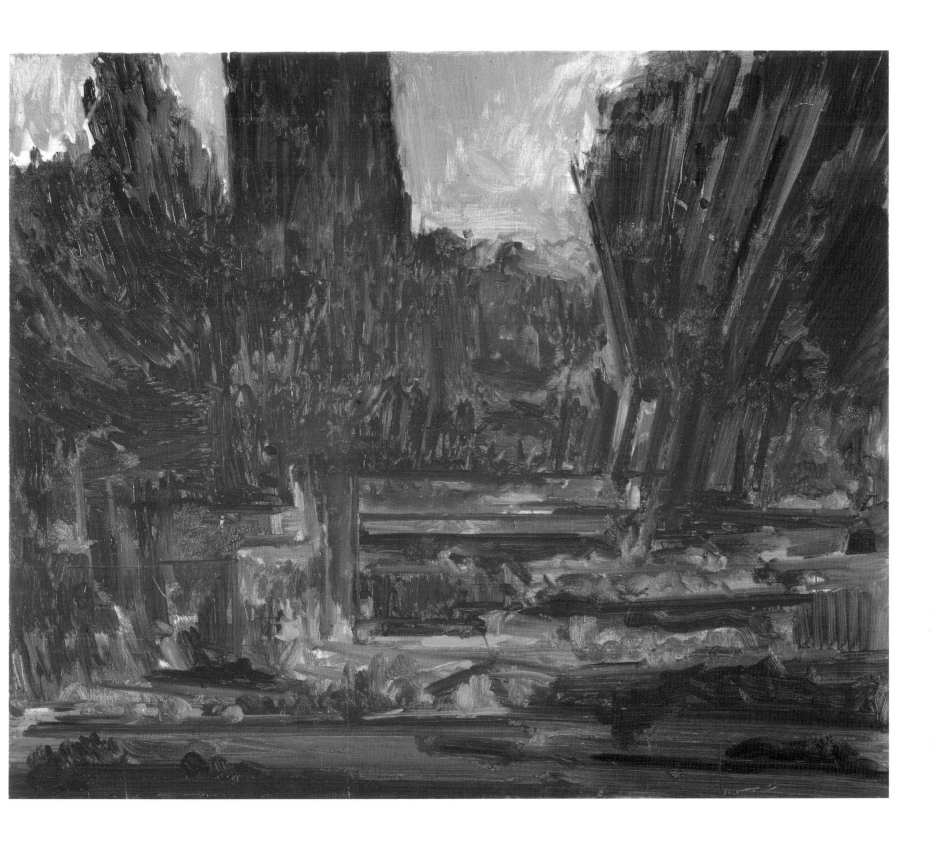

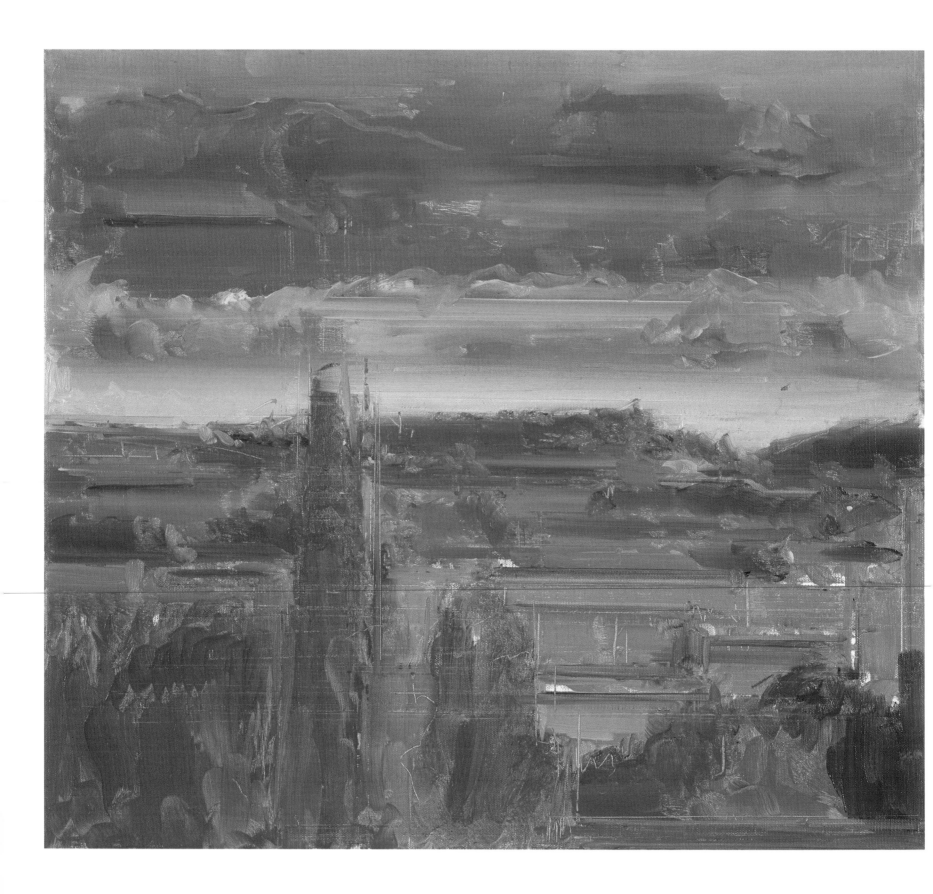

CHAPTER THIRTY-THREE

eading through these pages, it seems to me that I may have been too preoccupied with writing and myself, and not enough with people and events. It's true that my struggle with writing absorbed my entire conscious life, yet at the same time I was a husband, the father of three children, and surrounded by close friends. These sketches are by no means autobiographical, but are more a way of concentrating on one aspect of life: the place that Jerusalem has in my writing.

I haven't dealt with Jerusalem's history, nor with present-day Jerusalem, and not even with the essential problems of immigration, but rather with people like myself, who live in two worlds. For them, this duality both comprises a permanent mirror and intense self-examination: it is not an anomaly or a defect. Life's circumstances produced this duality, and is a like a hidden treasure for them.

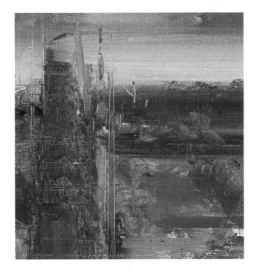

Immigration has sometimes been perceived of as a defect that needs to be "cured" or "fixed". This edifying view is very far from how I see it. Sometimes it is actually those people who were hurt who show us how to elevate life. A man who has suffered is more than just a social burden—sometimes he can be the source of feelings and thoughts that rise from the depths of the soul. The sidelines of society are no less important than the social center. And I would add: feelings and thoughts can crystallize on the sidelines, whereas the center, because of its tendency toward what is average and moderate, would reject them.

This time, too, I have not written directly about my mother and my father. My mother, as I've said, was murdered at the start of the war and later on I was separated from my father. After many years I was reunited with my father in Israel. My parents are part of me, to such an extent that I find it difficult to view them outside of me. They live in my imaginative writing as they were, and in the guise of other characters. But as for their tangible presence—of this I have not written. I find it hard to speak of them. Whenever I speak of them directly, it seems to me that I do them an injustice by speaking superficially or making inappropriate descriptions. I like to think that they live within my writing. And perhaps the day will come when I'll write about them with the right breadth, particularly my father, who was with me in his old age, and would visit me frequently in the cafés, and were it not for his closeness, it's doubtful that my memory would have gone to the places that it did.

Neither have I written about many close friends. Friendship is a delicate fabric between myself and them. It's hard to stick a pen in a place from where life still gushes out. Sometimes it seems to me that were it within my power to write about all the people among whom I lived, then my life would have been much fuller. But unfortunately, writing isn't a matter of choice. Years had to pass before I could find the words to write a novel about my parents, and more years until I could write about my grandparents. Writing is a slow process that cannot be hurried. Not that you could write about everything that you would like to. Every creative person, apparently, has his own turf, and woe betide him if he strays into an area that isn't his own.

Jerusalem, too, gave each of us something different. For quite a few of my friends who had been born in this city, it was sometimes the crown of their despair. I wasn't born here, but it's a city that has given me more than a city usually gives. Everything that had been snatched away from me so brutally in my childhood—I would rediscover here in Jerusalem. Sometimes I imagine myself doing exactly what my son Meir does: wander with an easel from one place in the city to another. Here's a wonderful tree, here a roof with an unusual slope or a street that climbs to the sky. Throughout the years I've been seeking out corners for writing in this city, and to my surprise—continue to find them. Had I ended up in another city, I doubt whether I would have become a writer.

Some years ago, I was lecturing in a town near Boston. A black woman who had been at my lecture came up to me and said with awe, "You're from Jerusalem! I'm seventy-five, and this is the first time that I'm looking at a man who's from Jerusalem." She stood opposite me astounded, as if I was not a human being but some marvel, and did not cease to say: "Good Heavens—you live in Jerusalem! I can't believe what I'm seeing!"

In that same city, I met with a Jewish professor of English literature, an educated, open-minded man. He questioned how I could live in Jerusalem, a city of religious zealots and fanatics. He had only visited it once, for a short time, but he had an arsenal of information, and was furious at the ultra-Orthodox, who "had made Jerusalem a backward city, mired in its medieval past."

The fifties and sixties were decisive; they proved to be formative years for me. The city and writing came together in me, and this link has lasted to this very day. Again and again I'm asked when I'm going to write about Israel. This question, which I was asked forty-five years ago, never goes away. It looks like it's going to haunt me till the end of my life. Once I couldn't restrain myself and I said, "I only write about Jerusalem. The Carpathian Mountains are also the Judean Hills. All the streets and all the cafés, even the trees and the flowers, everything that appears in my books—is Jerusalem."

It's hard to persuade people that a city is, among other things, a private matter. It molds everyone differently. Sometimes it is

actually the man in the street who instinctively picks up what journalists and professors don't see. The taxi drivers in Tel Aviv can immediately spot the Jerusalemite in me. Many years ago, in New York, I hailed a cab.

The driver turned around to me and said in Hebrew: "You're from Jerusalem?"
"What makes you think that?"
"Your bag, and the way you're holding it. I was a taxi driver in Jerusalem for ten years. I know who's from Jerusalem."

I was glad that he had recognized the city in me at a distance of thousands of miles.

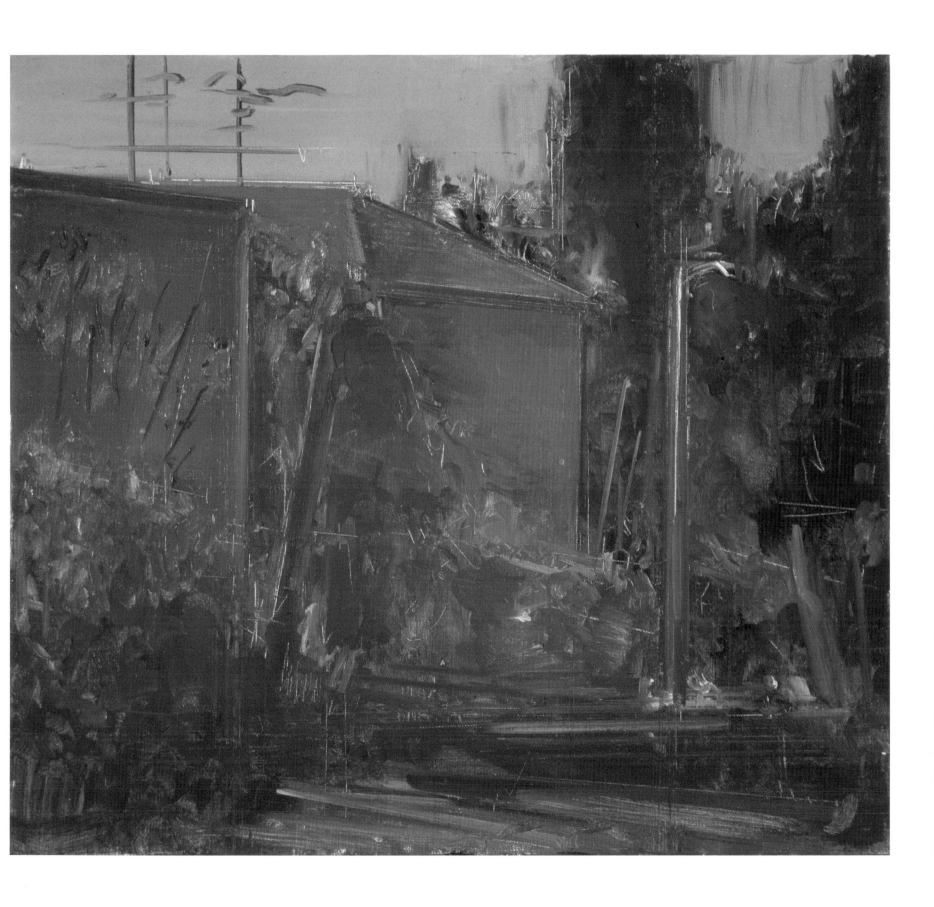

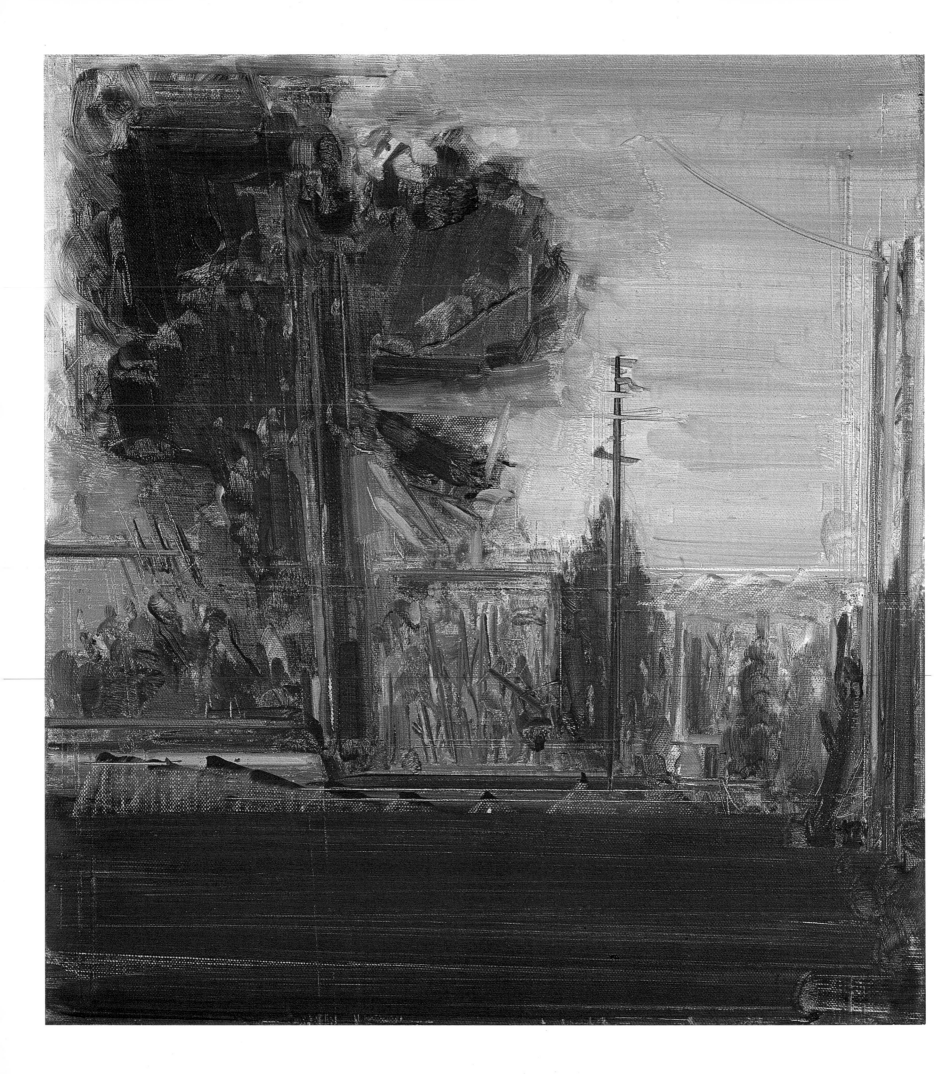

CHAPTER THIRTY-FOUR

All my books are essentially an inner conversation. This book was born out of a conversation with my son, Meir. After he returned from his studies in England, and began painting the landscape of Jerusalem, I suddenly felt the extent to which I'm bound up with this city. In 1998 I had returned to my birthplace, the city of Czernowitz, a journey that was punctuated with intense emotion. But even on the first day of my return, I knew that this city, with its pleasant streets, its gardens, the river and the parks—which are the marrow of my childhood and about which I have written so much—were no longer mine. I wouldn't have stayed there any longer than the allotted time. The city where I was born exists only in my imagination.

Between what exists there, and between my imagination, there is nothing that binds the two. I had taken away with me all that I held dear and replanted it in Jerusalem. This feeling is one that I have already been living with for many years, but it was only on my return from the city of my birth that it could be formulated.

My son Meir started to paint at a very early age. When he was thirteen, he illustrated my novel *Badenheim 1939*. His paintings speak my language. If I knew how to paint, I would paint like him. Sometimes it seems as if we're working along parallel lines—what he paints, I write. There is also a surprising similarity to our Jerusalem. I would perhaps express this by what it's *not*: it's not a display of the spectacular; it's not the historical in the usual sense of this word; it's not the sensational, not the original at any price; it's not an excess of emotion rather than form. It is steady observation from the sidelines of life, from where a simple beauty emerges.

These reflections have been a kind of confession about specific places and people; in other words, a religious attitude to life. When I say "religious" I mean seriousness and a sense of obligation to art. I believe art is about creation—and not about the ego, or making an impression, or exuding a sense of superiority toward others. But it is all about calling forth feelings that connect with other people.

Art that does not extend love, devotion, identification—cannot be meaningful art. By saying this, I don't imply a sentimental, sanctimonious, or overly emotional relationship to life. Art that has religious reverence carries with it harshness and discipline; the anarchic and the arbitrarily subjective are sometimes the enemy that destroys art from within. When I say a religious attitude, I mean the belief that inside every person, landscape, and still life, there is hidden a noble beauty.

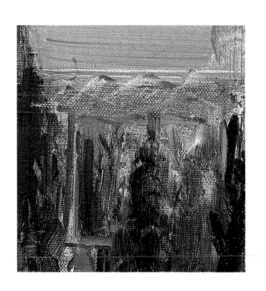

PAINTINGS AND DRAWINGS

Aharon Appelfeld, born in 1932 in Czernowitz, Bukovina (now part of Ukraine), is one of Israel's most celebrated novelists. A Holocaust survivor, he made his way to Italy and immigrated to Israel in 1946. Appelfeld's work is recognized worldwide as being among the most profound literary explorations of the Holocaust, and has met with international critical and popular acclaim. Appelfeld has received the Israel Prize, is a winner of America's National Jewish Book Award, and in October 2004 was awarded the Prix Médici Etranger, France's top literary award.

Meir Appelfeld was born in Jerusalem in 1965, where he attended classes in its Conservatory. It was subsequently his ambition to become a professional violinist. Once he had completed his army service, however, he decided on a radical change of direction and entered the Byam Shaw School of Art in London. After four years, he was accepted to the graduate school of the Royal Academy for Art, London, where he studied until 1994. He has since exhibited widely in Israel and abroad, and lectures at the Bezalel School of Art. He lives in Jerusalem.

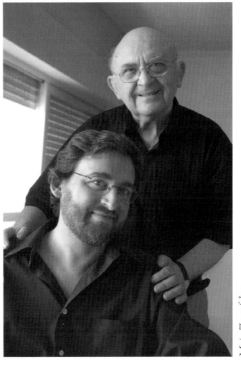

Meir Zarofsky

The Toby Press publishes fine writing, available at leading bookstores everywhere.
For more information, please visit www.tobypress.com